A True Source of Wonderment

From Earth Day to Earth Tomorrow

Robert Lundahl

Introduction- Bloody Thursday

Courtesy Arte Util

Initiator(s)

Inhabitants of Berkeley

Description

People's Park is a park located near the University of California. The University bought this plot of land containing residences for future development into student housing, parking, and offices. However, they ran out of funds leaving the lot only partially cleared of demolition debris and rubble.

After years of abandonment, local merchants and residents held a meeting to discuss possible uses and presented a plan for developing the under-utilized land into a public park. An article was published in a local counter-culture newspaper, to call for help from local residents. On Sunday, April 20, 1969, over 100 people arrived at the site to begin building the park, contributing trees, flowers, shrubs.Free food was provided, and community development of the park proceeded. The park was essentially complete by mid-May but Berkeley Vice Chancellor released plans for a sports field to be built on the site. Governor Ronald Reagan considered the creation of the park a direct leftist challenge to the property rights of the university and he sent 300 police officers into People's Park.

The officers cleared the area around the park destroying a large section of what had been planted and a perimeter chain-link wire fence was installed to keep people out. About 3,000 people congregated nearby UC Berkeley for a rally to discuss the Arab–Israeli conflict and, responding spontaneously, moved down toward People's Park.

The protesters were met by the remaining 159 police officers assigned to guard the fenced-off park. The huge clash was called Bloody Thursday, it finished with more than one hundred residents and police agents

injured, hundreds of protesters
arrested, one student blinded and one dead. On May 30, 1969, 30,000 Berkeley citizens secured a city permit and marched without incident past the barricaded People's Park to protest Governor Reagan's occupation of their city, the death of James Rector, the blinding of Alan Blanchard, and the many injuries inflicted by police.

The protests and demonstrations continued for two years. In 1972, the Berkeley City Council voted to lease the park site from the university. The Berkeley community rebuilt the park, mainly with people working for free and donated materials. Various local groups contributed to managing the park during the rebuilding. Today, People's Park is a free public park.

Clifforde Humphrey

Chapter One- A True Source of Wonderment

Robert Lundahl, Filmmaker, Journalist

Today, we take a step back in time, to the 1960s, and then strangely, further onward ahead into our new world of climate uncertainty, yet in that spirit of the first Earth Day, and a generation of logical dreamers who wanted to heal the planet before it was too late. We look back and we look ahead with Clifford Humphrey, who became the first curbside recycler, while still a student at UC Berkeley in 1968, and shortly thereafterModesto, California, where the business really took off. The life force of the planet, rebuilding our home world with Cliff Humphrey.

Cliff Humphrey, Visionary

I'm Clifford Humphrey, founder with my wife. We founded Ecology Action while I was a student at UC Berkeley, and I went to school originally to go into psycholinguistics. I wanted to know the history of language and learn how to make language really work for me, as to have an interest in the vocabulary that I was exchanging with audiences as I gave talks from Ecology Action's existence.

Then, as I went further into my Berkeley required courses, I discovered this intense interest in the life force, and how it was being not attended to, how it was being violated by the harvesting of minerals and trees from the Earth's surface. No thought about where we were all going. Back in 1968 through 74 or 75, the place was in a rush.

You know, there's all kinds of opinions about who was this or that, including who was a communist or not a communist, a socialist or a democrat or an independent. Firm opinions and a lot of arguments, but nobody really knew where we were going. And so, I was of such a personality, I backed off and didn't join in any of the arguments.

Peter Canejo became a figure later on. I believe he was a vice president with what's the author of Nader, Unsafe at Any Speed. I went to San Diego where I had lived, investigating where a convention was going to be. Well, the guy who was coming from Vietnam was assassinated, so that AP convention was called up. That's how fast things were moving in the 60s. They were really, really moving.

I want to tell you all out there, sitting still today, that I have experienced such a speed of development back in the 60s, and in my efforts to develop ecology action into a national movement. We decided to make it an organic force rather than a bureaucracy with a headquarters. So, we encouraged everyone to go their own way in a consistent way to preserve and understand the life force of the planet, but not to have any bureaucracy that needed a lot of funding.

Let's see, these things slip my mind. I haven't thought for a long time. Hotel Del Coronado, a wonderful, wonderful hotel. They were going to have us a guest speaker like an associated press convention. The head of the government from Vietnam was going to be a most interesting program for all of us at Berkeley at that time. So, I go down there to do a preliminary report on what we were going to do about his involvement.

And so, I did a lot of writings. I did a couple of tours, a combination of by bus and by train and by thumb, together around the country, couch surfing, of course. I call it, today I'm calling it the dirty fingernail approach because my future program I call the pollinator project.

And maybe we can talk some more about that as we go forward today. But I'm looking ahead to a revived earth movement. Over here, I have a planet on its axis.

And so, I can show students where they go when they go to sleep and it gets dark. It's not that the sun went down, it's that the planet spun around. And this apparatus is on casters.

And so, I wheel it around the classroom. And I can show you that half of the year when you go to breakfast, you are in an ascending configuration. And half the year when you go to breakfast, you are in a declining configuration.

People find this sometimes unbelievable and they'll turn away. But it is true as our planet orbits the sun with its axis always pointing at the north star, which happens to

be the end of the little dipper, which is upside down also. So, as we do that, half the time when you're going to breakfast, you're ascending and half the time going to breakfast, you're descending.

And you can prove this to yourself just by having a globe and walking around a light source. So, you can see that this is true as we orbit the sun. These truths and so, my hope is that this, you might say that the tail end of my career of ecology action, that as we understand more of where we live, we'll understand the wonderment of it.

It's all choked up already. The wonderment of it and take better care of the earth and its wonderment. And realize that as far as we know, we are alone in the cosmos except for God.

Can we say that? Is that a thing we could agree upon? And by the way, in water, I had one amazing moment sitting on the edge of a swimming pool with water.

I

 could feel the water coming into the pool on my ankles and feet. And I dally there feeling this water massage, you might say, a hydrologic treatment. And I came to have some wonderment of water.

I wonder as water, all life requires water. So, is water more than just water? Is there some kind of spirituality that water brings to us?

At least it brings to us a contemplation of all the movement that is going on. I'm getting overcome with my own rap here. But I have sat in the woods, say a point of observation, not in the woods, but looking out upon the woods, seeing the creek below me, trees and bushes and birds, maybe even a salamander or two.

Realizing that all have water. So, water is, I think we're supposed to be what, 90% water or something like that. And we are beholden to water.

And that, in my world, gives it at least a spiritual aspect. And we might come upon to hold water in a higher degree than just a spiritual aspect. It is a creative force and so on and so forth.

And it may be that we have made a mistake of worshiping competing doctrines, rather than realizing how simple an approach to the God force can be. I wish to make this part of my elders, if you will, proclamation as I gather up my experiences and begin to move onward. But the Pollinator Project, we're going to have a re-greening of the earth.

We're going to realize we've made some mistakes. And so, the one thing we have to

do is take care of the pollinators, who were like the leading force of regeneration of the planet. And so, I hope to introduce that here.

Of all things, the place called Truth or Consequences. I will introduce this concept in Truth or Consequences in my own backyard. I have two ravines that would be very expensive housing lots to develop.

But I shall plant pollinator seeds there and film how they go. And of the little group that I have here in TRC to work with. And I would encourage you, wherever you might be in the world, to think of this Pollinator Project of making sure that we have those bugs, everything from butterflies to bats to migrating birds, to be fed and be healthy.

And they can help pollinate the plants we need to have a green and healthy planet.

Robert Lundahl, Filmmaker, Journalist

Wow. And can you give me an example? You had this wonderful example of like places that we don't often look at.

You know, like these little corners where one road meets another and there's a water. Yes. You know, collection.

Clifford Humphrey, Visionary

Many of you realize we like to mow the sides of the road. We theoretically, I believe, do that. So when folks who are smoking throw out their cigarette, we don't get a fire.

Well, it's also a trough for the water. And here in New Mexico, you go out on the drive on the country roads, and you realize that the growth on the inside of the curve, the highway slants down to the inside of the curve. And so that little trough gets more water than the outside of the curve.

And by golly, it's greener all the time. And so, yes, that is one of the areas where pollinator seeds can just be distributed. And the natural water and rains will bring them down to the ground.

And some of them will sprout. So we are going to do this. It will be my policy, at least for the ones that I'm with here in New Mexico, to plant a stake of white, probably a two by four, and drive it down to maybe only a foot coming up and put a number on it.

And we're going to keep records of the pollinator habitat that we have befriended. And we'll just see how it goes. And I expect a lot of the plants selected will have blossoms.

And so we'll have everything from the wild bees to the migrating butterflies coming through and feeding on these plants. And I hope to start it. And I expect the same positive reactions that I experienced before with recycling when it became clear that that is the proper thing to do, to put your glass and cans and newspapers out on the curb.

Ecology Action, Recycling, Modesto, CA

And we started that first program in a place called Modesto, California. And that's where all the Gallo wine bottles are made. And we had markets from a firm that made the blow-in insulation in the attic.

That was out in Oakdale. And they would fireproof the ground and newsprint, and then blow it in the attics for insulation. And since we had canneries in Modesto, they had a lot of spilled cans and leftover can stock.

And so we could just add our tin cans and bimetal cans along with them. And then I went to Hayward and negotiated a market for the... What was that?

With metals, I think it was. Yes, metals, aluminum. And we would grind up the

cans.We blew the ground up cans into a 40-foot container, a 40-foot long container full of aluminum cans. That's a lot of cans. So in Modesto, we had drop-off, we had buy-back, and we had collection routes.

So drop-off, buy-back, and collection routes throughout Modesto and Turlock. We got recycling on post-consumer waste, it's called. We got it going.

Ecology Action

And it was the right thing to do. And thousands of folks joined in. So I'm hoping the same thing will happen with the pollinator project.

We'll have groups of three or four people all riding together now. No taking a convoy of cars out to scratch up a little dirt, you know. We're going to go out and scratch up some dirt and throw out the seeds to make sure the pollinators are happy as they do their part of re-greening the planet Earth.

So that's, I'm tipping my hat and encouraging people to get ready to take on this pledge of the dirty fingernail project of the Earth. I don't know whether I'll pledge, whether I'll make myself part of Earth Day or not. This activity does not have to wait for a special da To some extent, it'll be rigged to coincide with when you get your rains. We want to get them out there, get the seeds in the ground. And right now I'm working with a thing called the Johnson Sue Digester being developed here in New Mexico.

And that is a process of digesti

ng organic material for a year without turning it. It's a

technique that can be found on the internet, Johnson Sue Biodigesters. And that also yields you a liquid product besides the normal thing of a compost product.

And this liquid product we can use to pre-coat the seeds that we plant for these plants that the digesters feed on for a good beginning, a good start of their growth. So we're looking forward to publicizing the pollinator plots and the pre-treatment of the seeds. We hope that will advance, you could say, home agriculture's return.I remember for World War II, we had victory gardens. You remember that?

Robert Lundahl, Filmmaker, Journalist

I was growing up in the late 50s and the early 60s. And my dad composted and we had gardens. He taught me how to garden when I was seven years old.

I thought that was pretty interesting.Cliff Humphrey

I got in trouble, Robert, for eating the carrots while they were still young and very juicy. I just love that.

Robert Lundahl, Filmmaker, Journalist

It's a fabulous way for youth to figuratively put their hands in the soil, but all that that brings is remarkable. That's right. And so after you've been a few rounds and a few seasons and a few gardens, you start to become more and more amazed.

Cliff Humphrey

I grew up in Pasadena and we ate avocados on white bread still up in the tree.

Robert Lundahl, Filmmaker, Journalist

Wow.

Cliff Humphrey

Yeah, we would hope our folks wouldn't catch us up there, but sometimes we'd get careless and drop the bread loaf down on the ground and we'd get caught. They weren't terribly upset, but it was possible to be distracted squeezing avocados onto white bread in a tree to fall out of the tree, but we never did. We enjoyed eating it, yes.

Robert Lundahl, Filmmaker, Journalist

That's wonderful. Where did you live in Pasadena?

Cliff Humphrey

All I can remember for sure was on Flower Street, north of Colorado, and it was one wonderful street that went north into the hills on both sides of the street with great big green trees. I'm sure some of the viewers will know what street I'm talking about. And I must say that my mom and her sister decorated floats for the Rose Parade.

It was different than being so commercialized as it is now. But we had great fun up there setting up the step ladders and the planks. And then the adults would join us before the parade actually started.

We had many offers of money to let others sit on it, but they were teasing us kids because they knew that we'd brought them up for the family. Yes. My father and his brothers were all into agriculture and they knew that the orange trees were getting woody, they called it. I didn't know from the smog or what, but we had that as a family

consciousness when we moved north to Paradise. where I saw my first movie, Swiss Family Robinson. I remember that experience to this day.

Of all things, I was right down in the front left-hand seat staring up at Swiss Family Robinson as part of my very early education, which I'm sure an anthropologist could probably figure out exactly what aspects of my interests were inspired by Swiss Family Robinson. But in Paradise, California, I also met a miner who was walking on a back road behind where we lived. And he was a remarkable friend to us kids.

We actually sat down with him and he told us about gold mining with a pan and water. And so I became an amateur gold panner from that talk and collected my own pan and knew how to put it in the fire to blue it. The bluing of the pan in the fire, just like you make it a cook pan, you might say, and you blew it to make sure there's no oil of any kind left.

And so you swirl the around and pretty soon there's a tail of the gold coming out of the black sand. That really influenced me as a kid that I could mine gold and be part of the history of Sutter's Mill and so on and so forth in California history. And I'll tell you this because it's one thing I've never done and maybe some of our listeners might want to do it. I've never gone into a corrugated drain pipe. The pipes that go under our road, y know. It's a natural, what would we call it?

Sluice box. It's a natural sluice box for black sand entrapment. And it could be that there's literally a fortune.

When I did my gold panning, it was gold controlled economy at $35 an ounce. And so I used to carry a little glass vial and I finally gave it all away at $35 an ounce. It wasn't like over a thousand.

I think today it's almost $2,000 an ounce. And so I would suggest to you that might be my pleasure and be the first ones to go out and mine these corrugated drain pipes. Just sweep all of the debris out.

And the hint of riches to follow through to you would be if there's any black sand in these corrugated drain pipes. And if you find black sand in them, sweep them all or vacuum them even clearly and have fun panning out the gold. It's a lot of fun too.

I just can't tell you how exciting that might be for you to pan that gold out of these drain pipes. Valuable, but it's also a beautiful, beautiful thing to pan gold. I'll pass that along as a maybe possible valuable comment I make today to you.

Robert Lundahl, Filmmaker, Journalist

With regard to the Pollinator Project, like how do you engage youth groups? And are you engaged in youth groups? And here you are telling this beautiful story of what it's like to be outdoors, which is something that we should share with our youth more today.

But to answer the question, are you reaching out to youth groups to become expert pollinators?

Cliff Humphrey

No, not yet. But you, that's a very, as you've heard a lot of you hear me say, oh my, that's a very good question. I don't know why I haven't done that, but that is a wonderful idea.

And I assure you, as I go forward, I will. I will reach out to youth groups. I think that a lot of parents, maybe I'll find out that there's a fear.

There's, for instance, here in TRC, we've just passed the money to actually put a fence around the high school, a cyclone fence. And there's going to be a great control over who comes and who's able to leave. Right now, as you know, the high school crowd is into driving around.

The older students have cars and they like to flee the campus for the restaurants. And I don't know if a clamping down is the right thing to do. I would be encouraging more field trips, I think, if I was associated with schools.

And like this, what is this model? I got to get used. Yes, this model here is the foot diameter globe mounted on its axis.

The axis always points at the last star, which is the North Star in the Little Dipper. And because then–how can I show you here? Because I'm going to have trouble with this, aren't I?

In other words, the orbit is always pointing to the same location. It's not like a ball circling the planet. It's different.

It's a special kind of orbit with the axis pointing at the North Star. And so half the time you're going down to breakfast and half up to breakfast. And that's the part of this lecture you can take to heart, if you will, and try that in your house and realize there's a truth to it.

And my belief is that if we understand more of, let's say, the astronomical aspects of our homeland, we'll come to have a better respect for it because it's a true source of wonderment.

Chapter Two- Why The Native Nations Have Been So Successful Lowell Bean, PhD Anthropologist

One of the reasons that the—one of the many reasons that the Native American people could live as well as they did and have complex social organizations was because they managed the land in a way to take care of it so it would always support them well. So a principal value, you don't take everything. You always leave something behind.

If there are ten deer, you don't kill ten deer. You kill what you need at the moment. With the—with trees, for example, you may trim them in such a way so that they weren't overgrown.

And I've got whole essays on this sort of thing. Piñon would be an example. Acorn.

Cactus. You made sure that there was going to be something for the future. And you took what you needed and you stored it and you could take piñon and cactus buds and acorns and mesquite beans and so forth in great quantities without damaging the future of the plant.

And you could store them in huge baskets and containers of one sort or another. Ceramics or baskets. The other factor was you shared your—you shared this wealth with other Cahuilas or other IndiaSo there could be a surplus down here and there Who

Mojave Bird Singers, Who Are My People? Film, Robert Lundahl

could be a shortage up at Morongo. And then the ceremonial—ceremonial duties, if you will, required that any group going to the ceremony of another group or maybe even
a social visit, you brought that which you had a surplus of to give as a gift to the other people. So if the mesquite is short up here, it might be locked down at Indio and you'd have your ceremony and those people would bring these foods together.

And after the ceremonies were over, the nets would get together and they would divide the food that was brought to the ceremonial house and give to people with that which they needed. So you're short on mesquite, someone else wasn't, so you got some mesquite or acorn or piñon or whatever it was. So there was this interchange of the basic economics—economic resources of the community going on regularly.

So is that one of the reasons that you're saying that tribes can come together well over issues because there's been this exchange ongoing? Yeah. There was always this inter-tribal, inter-tribal exchange of economic assets. And if it wasn't—it wasn't just food that was traded, okay, so you're short of food. You make—your ladies make up a bunch of really nice baskets and maybe the men make some tools and you bring the tools and the baskets to the ceremony and that's a signal, aha, they need food. So there you go. And you think about it, every time there's a death, this goes on.

These ceremonies for the dead lasted a week and you had to feed a lot of people, so there had to be a lot of food. But what was left over then was divided and it went where it ought to go. It was a brilliant, sophisticated system.

And you know, people used to say Indians are simple? Hardly.

Chapter Three- The 9000 Year History of the Oasis of Mara

Pat Flanagan

Pat Flanagan is a longtime compadre and friend and informal co-writer.

She's a scientist, a botanist, a biologist, naturalist and educator. Pat tells the story, the only story, the big story of humans and the environment. How people first got here, what they found, and why it matters today.

In light of global heating, I made a documentary film about it. The desert, its ecological and cultural vulnerabilities. And it's called, Who Are My People?

Pasadena Train Station, Who Are My People? Film, Robert Lundahl

Who Are My People Film

Flocks of snowbirds came to Southern California by train, to what was then regarded as a sort of heaven on earth. They had come from congested and polluted places like Chicago and Detroit. Disembarking in Pasadena to the Green Hotel.

Green Hotel, Pasadena, Who Are My People? Film, Robert Lundahl

And they instigated and demonstrated the mobility of the era. Recognizing the sanctity of the environment due to their ability to move about. My mother and father arrived in Pasadena in 1936.

Archa A. Lundahl/Robert Lundahl {Baby}

When I was born, my mom said, I'm taking him to the desert where the air is clean. The trips to the desert were usually made in the spring, down Foothill Boulevard, wrapping around the San Bernardinos and over the Cajon Pass. Foothill was special.

Foothill Drive In, Azusa, CA, Who Are My People? Film, Robert Lundahl

It was the last segment of Route 66 heading into LA. So it stood to reason, this was the way out. If Pasadena was becoming Detroit, we would keep moving.

Industrial Film, Shell Oil, Narrator

And as the road cut through the broad plains, you felt the tremendous space all around you. The country rolling out to the horizon, and you rolling with it.

Who Are My People? Film

After World War II, returning GIs
witnessed consumer democratization. With automobiles now the preferred way of travel, the motel provided affordability on the road. And Foothill was a parade of motel wonders.

Industrial Film, Shell Oil, Narrator

The road like river water was running under you.

Wigwam Motel, Foothill Blvd. Who Are My People? Film, Robert Lundahl 29 Palms Inn, 2012, Who Are My People? Film, Robert Lundahl

29 Palms Inn

Who Are My People? Film

But we would head to 29 Palms, where the inn beckoned.

Industrial Film, Shell Oil, Narrator

You sort of sense the real meaning behind the word, *freedom*.

Robert Lundahl, Filmmaker, Journalist

In post-war America, there were kids everywhere. And they congregated too. One such family, the Johansings, who owned a refuge for the traveler called the 29 Palms Inn.

Fate had chosen them to be the custodians and stewards of a 9,000-year-old refuge. At that time, long ago, I met a rapidly changing landscape inhabited by early indigenous peoples to the Americas, following the last ice age. It is here our story begins.

Can you talk about your connection with the inn and the Oasis of Mara, and how it all began for you?

Pat Flanagan

It all began for me in a very thin thread. Because back when I was like a sophomore in high school, it was an all-girls school. We were having a dance.

And I told my brother he had to take Jane Johansing to the dance. Jane became the owner. Her family was the ownership of the 29 Palms Inn.

They went to the dance. Then history goes on. And ultimately, in the 90s, they got married.

And in 2002, I was deciding, well, what am I going to do when I move out to the desert

from San Diego? And I decided I didn't know enough about the Mojave, so I better go there, and for other reasons as well. So then I moved there.

And I became very involved with finding out about the history of the Oasis of Mara. And a lot was going on. And so that's how I got into it.Sort of through marriage, but first introducing my brother to the woman who, when she got older, became the owner. And they're in the fifth generation now. So that's how that worked.

That make sense?

Oasis of Mara, Who Are My People? Film, Robert Lundahl
Oasis of Mara, Who Are My People? Film, Robert Lundahl

Robert Lundahl, Filmmaker, Journalist

And you have played an important role there, taking guests around and looking at the land and the features and this amazing place that people wouldn't suspect, maybe, or understand at first glance.

Pat Flanagan

I think that's correct. Since I've been doing this since 2002, I've had more opportunity than many who might give tours out here to involve myself in research that is done, such as the geology and the trench that was dug. So we know how old it is.

And just the history as it's come down through the ages and been written about.

Robert Lundahl, Filmmaker, Journalist

Well, we should probably back up a little bit because we talked about the inn. And you segued to the oasis, which is on the property of the inn. And the inn was, I guess, brought into being in about the early 1940s or late 1930s, something like that.

Is that correct?

Well, the inn was the first business in Twentynine Palms. And it is on one end of the Oasis of Mara.

Who Are My People? Film, Robert Lundahl

Pat Flanagan

And if you go back in history a little bit, quite a bit, as a matter of fact, it was the homeland for the Serrano Indians. And the Serrano lived there for generations. And the Chemehuevi, who are southern Paiutes, moved in with them.

And they were living very compatibly together. And then things started happening that they were unaware of because the federal government sent out a survey, the Washington Survey, to do the baseline. And at that time, they interviewed the people at the Oasis when they were in Twentynine Palms.

They filed with the federal government their report, and it included the Serrano people as being on a reservation. It belonged to the Indians. So that happened. And then, later on, the state of California asked the federal government if they could have the Oasis. And the federal government knew better, but the federal government said, sure. So they gave it to the state of California, who then sold it to the Southern Pacific Railroad.

And nobody was really paying any, I mean, they were not telling the Indians about this. They continued to live there. And it was only much later that the Southern Pacific Railroad sold it to a man named Roberts, who ultimately sold it to two of his partners, of which the Johansing was one of those partners.

And that was in, I think, 1939. In 1928, they split their ownership up, and the Inns stayed with Johansing. And that's how the Johansing family has been there five generations, ever since, and how I got attached to it. But it's Indian land initially.

Robert Lundahl, Filmmaker, Journalist

Well, as we talked about, my family was going out there pretty early, and we were talking about the circumstances of that. But my family and my mother's sister's family loved it and went out there. And my grandfather was somehow involved, and

recognized the sacredness of the place and the importance of the Indian cultures.

And that must have been, well, I think it was wartime. It was World War II era. So it might have been 42, 43, something like that.And then the first pictures I have were

1948. Of my cousin Jody out there, Aunt Alice, And they enjoyed it, and were really taken by the land and the place and the culture.

So I was trying to kind of establish that date as being sometime in the 40s. And that was early then. So that was after the beginning.

It must have been pretty rough and ready at that point.

Pat Flanagan

By the 1940s, I think there was a sign on the front of the property since 1928. And so lots has happened in that period of time. But yeah, by the 1940s, when I was sort of just born, they were ramping up.

And that's sort of when Jane was just born too.

Robert Lundahl, Filmmaker, Journalist

Yeah. Well, a lot of people don't know what an oasis is. And here we have one out in the desert, just east of Los Angeles.

And there are several more major oases, which we probably don't want to locate or talk about. But that's one that's available, you know, on the road. And it's a public place.

And it's a business. And a beautiful garden. And so many attributes that it has. So what

is an oasis?

Pat Flanagan

Well, I ask people that almost always. And they say, well, it's a place with water. But then you say, well, how did the water get there?

And in this case, if you look on a map, you will see a mile-long straight line. And that is the vegetation that follows the Pinto Mountain Fault. And because of the work that Ana Cadena did as a geologist, graduate student, putting a trench across the fault, we know that about 9,000 plus years ago, the earth moved.

And when it moved, it interfered with the drainage, which was going down to where the Marine base is now, and set up rigs of water and formed a sag pond. And that became the beginning of the oasis. And sag ponds are sort of very shallow ponds formed on fault lines.

So do you want me to go on with that?

Robert Lundahl, Filmmaker, Journalist

So to paint the picture, we have the inn, which is a collection of cabins, essentially, these days. And the main building that houses a restaurant and a beautiful swimming pool.

It's a lot of fun to sit around there and have a lemonade or something. And it's very beautiful and accommodating to tourists. And then the oasis itself is, well, you said it's on one end.

Joshua *Tree National Park, PHOTO: Robert Lundahl, 2012*

Pat Flanagan

It's on one end. And you could walk from there to what used to be the visitor center for the National Park, but that's now been moved to another location in some new development in the city. But you still can walk across that oasis and follow it.

Robert Lundahl, Filmmaker, Journalist

And yeah, and I remember the park headquarters when it was there. I mean, I remember that from being a kid. I don't remember that from the last 10 years or 15 years.So I don't know when they moved. But it was there. Yeah.

And there's a row of palms along that fault line. And I don't remember if there's 29 of them or whether there's more or less.Pat Flanagan

Well, the palms are interesting. There's all these stories about, oh, somebody counted them and said there were 29. And then there's another one that said the tribal people were told by their god to move there because they would have more male children.

And the first year they planted, and every male child, they planted a palm. And that was, they gave us the 29 palms. The palms that are there is the most northwesterly grove of the Washingtonian fan palms that begin down in Baja, California in the central canyons.

Oasis of Mara

And probably, you know, they could have gotten there, could have been the tribal people planted them for sure. They could also have been brought by birds that eat the dates or by coyotes that eat the dates that the birds don't get. And then they, of course, poop out the seeds. So one way or the other.

Robert Lundahl, Filmmaker, Journalist

So this is pretty amazing then. So there's a fault line and the earthquake and the water at that point. You told me a story about what happened when the earthquake occurred from the Serrano perspective.

Pat Flanagan

I think the Serranos, that was, if you look back 9,000 years, and they weren't called Serranos then, but there have been people living in the desert. As far as I know, and the data could be more updated now, 13,500 years in the region. And as the ice ages were ending, the springs that had nourished the people with water, as well as the lakes, were drying up.

And so life was beginning to look, oh my goodness. And all of a sudden, you get this opening and you get water coming to the surface and forming this sag pond, which is, of course, going to bring in the animals that they can then, by living a little bit aways, they can hunt those animals and get food. Plus it's water, so plants can grow there and feed them.

So it was fortuitous.

Robert Lundahl, Filmmaker, Journalist

And today that pond is still there. It's a body of water surrounded by palms.

Pat Flanagan

But it's not a mile long. Now it is much smaller, way smaller. The aquifer is getting way down there, but the palm trees along that mile that still have roots that can get into the water surface water are growing.

If you look at a map, you can see that line. And there's other plants too. There's like the mesquite, the honey mesquite that's growing along there that gives it its look.

Honey Mesquite

Robert Lundahl, Filmmaker, Journalist

Mm-hmm, which is an edible legume.

Pat Flanagan

Definitely, and a great agricultural plant because you don't have to plant it. You only have to harvest.

Robert Lundahl, Filmmaker, Journalist And a staple for the tribal people even today.

Pat Flanagan

Absolutely.

Robert Lundahl, Filmmaker, Journalist

There's so much to talk about here. Well, next to the end, you mentioned the Serranos and the Chemehuevis who came to live amicably in that area with them. Next to the end, there's an old Chemehuevi cemetery.

Pat Flanagan

Yes.

Robert Lundahl, Filmmaker, Journalist

And that was in use when? I mean, is it still in use?

Pat Flanagan

No, but when the state of California absorbed from the federal government the oasis, that cemetery was there then. So that's back in the 1800s. And then that cemetery is there today, but initially, it was cared for by the City of 29 Palms.

And then that has now been given back to the 29 Palms Band of Mission Indians. And so they are caring for it. And it is still there.

Robert Lundahl, Filmmaker, Journalist

Well, we've interviewed Matthew Leivas Sr. three times actually for KPFK. And we talked about water, the Colorado River, pollution, encroachment, industry, and the impacts that have occurred to the Colorado River area where the Chemehuevis have a reservation today. They are traditionally semi–nomadic, correct?

Pat Flanagan

I'm not sure that they would call themselves nomadic. I think they would hunt. They would have a place they lived in the wintertime and then a place they went to in the summer.

But I don't know that they call themselves nomadic.

Robert Lundahl, Filmmaker, Journalist

I see.

Pat Flanagan

They have stabilized places for time of year.

Robert Lundahl, Filmmaker, Journalist

Right. And the Salt Song trails that are a part of Chemehuevi life connect many of these places and other Southern Paiute villages and so forth. And they are mapped.They are mapped through song.

Pat Flanagan

Yes.

Robert Lundahl, Filmmaker, Journalist

And that's really amazing. So painting the broader picture of who are the people and how do they live, you know? And so water is extremely important.

Pat Flanagan

And that's one of the... The Oasis of Mara is on the Salt Song Trail. It's also interesting to know when I grew up, we were told that the Indians did not own land.That is incorrect out here. They did own land and their deed was a song. And if you wanted to know, go hunting, for instance, in a certain mountain range, you knew whose song said who owned it and you would go ask for permission.

So yes, those songs are extremely important.

Robert Lundahl, Filmmaker, Journalist

And so you're hinting that they're important to future land claims or future management involvement or all of our ways in which we interact with federal agencies and manage land and the role of the tribes and so forth. So this establishes the presence and as you said, the ownership.

Pat Flanagan

Well, it did, except that then paperwork took over. So that's before the Johansings ever got to the end. It had been decades since the paperwork had overridden the Indian claim.

They tried, but what happens with Washington? It didn't work out. The Smiley Commission that came around the latter part of the 1800s, they were told by the government that they should repatriate tribal people with their land, but they could recommend, but they had no real power.

They actually tried to get the Serrano-Chemehuevi people back at the oasis, but they weren't allowed to do so because we already had all this paperwork beginning. And so what they got was 160 acres to the south and which today, I think dating back to like 2014, they have built a casino and that is there and you can see it in there. So they're our neighbors now.

Robert Lundahl, Filmmaker, Journalist

Can we talk about the importance of water? I mean, we talked about the Salt Song trails connecting villages and important places and water sources. And I experienced this firsthand because I went to a sweat in a sweat lodge ceremony in Big Pine with a healer and an elder named Raymond Stone.

And he apparently was very well-known. Matthew Leivas knows him. And as an outsider, when I joined the sweat, there are songs sung.

And even though they were sung in Paiute, maybe it was just the moment, but I started to understand what the story was in the songs and the songs named springs and places and water sources. So where does that bring us today? When we look at the importance of water in a parched desert landscape and we consider that there are projects going on that people would like to do.I mean, one of them was like large-scale solar development in the desert and now another one is a water marketing scheme. Can you talk a little bit about that?

Pat Flanagan

Well, that's, as you say, and as Matt would tell you, water is life. The garden at the 29 Palms Inn is 2000 years old and it has been used for 2000 years and the water was indeed life. And now the water is not what it used to be.

You can ask any of the water agencies and the solar projects that go in, unfortunately, they don't, the large-scale ones, the utility scale, do not choose a landscape that has already been degraded. They choose pristine lands of which there's vegetation on the land and that vegetation we now know, as a matter of fact, the creosote, for instance, which has a space between it, but that space is just, what you don't see is underground is the miles and miles and depth of mycorrhizal fungi which absorbs and keeps carbon dioxide. So when they're scraping the land to put in their solar project, they're releasing carbon dioxide.

The group that I work with has just released a report on that. And nonetheless, as well, when the ice ages retreated and all of the dry lakes, which weren't dry then, they were wet before and during the ice ages, then they became dry. And then you have the winds that come from the west and they blow the dust.

And it's the plants, the creosote and the grass that keep what is called a linear dune stable. If you get rid of the vegetation, the dust blows. So that has been an offshoot of every single one of the solar projects that they have put in that downwind people have been physically harmed by the blowing dust.

You talk to the air quality management districts in the county as well, and you say, well, don't do this or you have to do what they do in the Owens Lake area, which is to put in four inches of crushed gravel over a mat to keep it in place. Well, that will cost a lot of money, right? So, but they will tell you when they give you the permit to do this from the water agency, they'll say, if they're blowing dust, you have to water it.

Okay, you water it. That's water that we don't have much of. And within the desert, the water evaporates.
So you need to water it many times a day. And it still evaporates. So we have places like Dagget and Newberry Springs that have been overwhelmed with dust.

Houses have been almost buried with dust. And then Lucerne Valley is the same way. You get this horrible dust blows. I get dust blows here from the original solar projects that went in Joshua Tree. I'm still getting that dust flying when the wind is blowing directly from the west. So the water is getting less.

The need to use it, although it's not very effective, is getting more. Is that clear?

Robert Lundahl, Filmmaker, Journalist

Yeah, and the population is going nuts. I mean, Riverside County is a really fast growing area in San Bernardino County as well. So this population pressure, I mean, certainly in my lifetime and yours, we've seen this process. And I made a film, which you know, called Who Are My People? That begins at the end. And it starts out by saying, first came people, then came cars, then came houses.

Who Are My People? Film Trailer, Robert Lundahl, 2014

And it was this process of development and encroachment. And the encroachment reminds me of the Willie Boy story. You know, that's about that time when the laws and the paperwork began to change and the tribal laws were no longer respected.

And so I'll just sort of leave that for the recording that Tell Them Willie Boy is here.

Pat Flanagan

The latest and best book that's been written by Cliff Trasker and it's called Willie Boy, The Last Western Manhunt. And that's got the real history based on multiple interviews with tribal people. And they knew stuff that others weren't willing to admit, namely that Willie Boy totally escaped and died in Pahrump of tuberculosis many years later.

I know from the Oasis because we have a Salt Song that is one of many Salt Songs that look at water sources and salt sources throughout four states. Back in 2003 was the first invitation to tribal members to the Oasis to meet actually with government people so they could sit down and talk collegially about things that are needed. We wanted to do that again.

And when they sang their Salt Songs on that night in 2003, it had been the first time in nearly a hundred years. In 2016, we had a gathering of tribes. They invited themselves back to bless the national monuments in 2017.This place is a place they've come to and we would like to set up for them to be able to come more with their Salt Songs because of the water.

Robert Lundahl

Yeah, and it's a place that's really integral to our understanding of California history and the history of the West. And if you look at a snapshot, you wanna teach this in elementary school or high school or something like that.
This is the whole story right here.

So going back to 24,000 years ago, you have peoples in Russia around Lake Baikal and Northern China, and they are not yet moving but we know who they are, who they were. And then about 15,000 years ago, following the melting of the great glaciers across North America, both of them, there's two large- Cordillera. Cordilleran.

And there's a question of how did people move? How did people move into this area that we call North America now and South America? And we had a conversation, well, apparently they populated both continents really fast.

There are sites in South America that are 14,800 years old, have dates of that. And some people dispute this or that, or this was found in a river, not in a place where there is a better analysis possible and so forth. But the overall picture seems to be that they moved and they moved early.

And that really began about 15,000 years ago when everything opened up and people dispersed widely. So that's the inland route. That's the coastal route.

That's however that occurred. And so when you're talking about people being in the desert for 13,000 years, there's the whole story right there. They're pretty early for North America.

And then you're talking about the oasis and the end of the ice age and the waters flowing and erupting and so forth, 9,000 years ago. So we have this fast commercial paced culture of most people listening in Los Angeles right now. And they wanna go to the movies or they gotta go down the freeway somewhere.

And we just forget these things. We don't realize it's not in the top of the mind really. And you're an educator.

What do you think about that?

Pat Flanagan

Well, I think that the stories have not been told often enough. And that's how it has to come. It can't come in sentences with little bullet points in front of it.

That this is the story. And there's many chapters to the story. And that's the value of coming to places just like the inn where you can hear the story and you can see the story.

Chapter Four–Blowout at Platform A

Robert Lundahl, Filmmaker, Journalist

This is a story of the early years of the oil industry, a burning river and a blowout. Earth Day and the Environmental Protection Agency and how it all intersects. We're back with David Pu'u, indigenous Hawaiian and lifelong surfer raised in Santa Barbara and the incredulous story of the birth of the environmental movement in the United States during the 1970s and how that leads us to regenerative practices today.

David Pu'u

Well, my parents moved from L.A. area, where my dad was working for all these military contractors, to Santa Barbara in about 1964, 1965. And so I grew up at the beach around South Bay, Newport, that whole area. You know, they have these beautiful white groomed beaches, no trash.

They rake the beaches every day, no real pollution or anything that was evident in the water. And the first thing I noticed when we got to Santa Barbara is, what's all this black gooey stuff that was tar? And it was kind of everywhere.

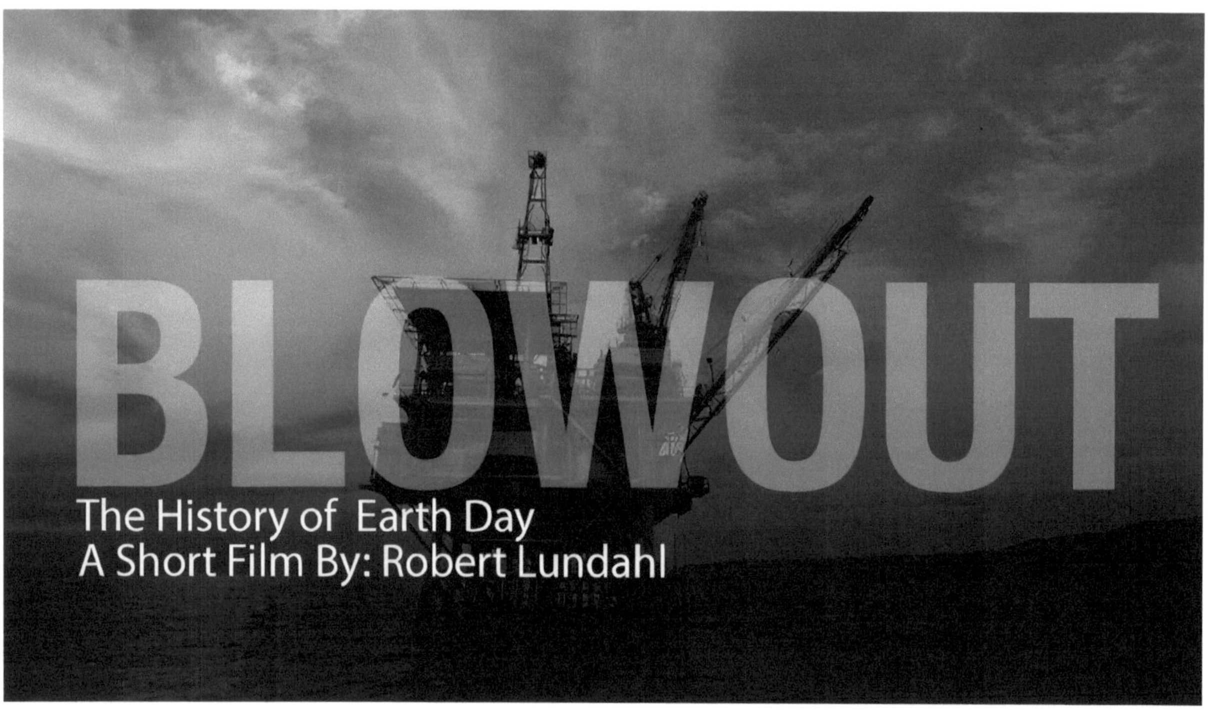

So it was quite a shock. I remember not liking it. You have all this sticky stuff to deal with just so you can go surfing.

And it took me a couple of years to kind of learn how to navigate around it to where it finally felt like, OK, this is home. This is where I'm going to grow up. This is where I'm going to serve.

Robert Lundahl, Filmmaker, Journalist

Tell me what you observed with regard to the industrial aspects of it and the oil drilling and the presence of larger oil seeping and eventually what happened with the blowout.

David Pu'u

Well, I grew up in Goleta, and so my home beach was a place called Sands, which sits atop a point called Coal Oil Point. And, you know, there's an incredible amount of natural seepage there just offshore of Coal Oil Point, maybe, oh, God, 75 yards out from the beach. You can actually see methane and asphaltum coming to the surface on some days.

And that's just the way it was. You knew it was time to leave when the wind went onshore and you got the smell of hydrocarbon come wafting across the waters and, yeah, time to go. Tar is going to come back in right as soon as we start smelling it.

And the wind would blow it in and you get out of the water to avoid becoming a sticky mess. It really became kind of an art, you know, how to avoid getting tar everywhere and having to clean your wax off and start all over again.

Robert Lundahl, Filmmaker, Journalist

Yeah, we were still in the era of the 50s in my family, my dad being military, Navy, and we'd go down to Huntington Beach and he'd be drinking Schlitz beer in the car and you'd just, like, toss him over his shoulder out onto the highway. You remember that where all the beer cans and everything were out on the highway?

David Pu'u

Oh, yeah. Yeah. One of the beaches that I frequented when I was really young was Tin Can Beach, which was up by Seal Beach, and there were cans everywhere.

Robert Lundahl, Filmmaker, Journalist

That's the one. That's the one where my dad's Schlitz cans went.

Robert Lundahl

But we had a Navy dad. He scared my brother to death one day when he took him down to Seal Beach. My brother thought that my dad was going to sign him up for the Navy and he cried and cried and cried and wanted to go home.

And, you know, it's one of those family stories. It was a different time. A couple of things hit the news and one was this blowout in the Santa Barbara Channel.

And you referred to the seepage. And I'll just jump ahead a little bit. What happened when they tried to shut it down is they had these two giant blocks of steel and they clamped them shut, the hole that they had drilled, you know, they needed to cap it or close it or slam it, slam the door on that, you know, so they tried to do that.

And then the oil came up and all these other seeps broke through the surface and the seafloor and five, six areas. And it was like completely out of control, you know, just and it went on for a long time. And I was in the news for a long time.

David Pu'u

Well, I remember that the oil presence became a lot more pervasive. There was just more of it. There are some days where there would just be, you know, a black wave extending a half mile, mile out to sea. And we'd never seen that much before. Although in the ship's log for Juan Cabrillo, his navigator noted that they were sailing through a black sea with fumes so heavy they

thought they might be overcome and perish. And it went on for miles and miles and miles.

And that was one of the first documented pieces of evidence of the amount of oil in the Santa Barbara Channel. It's, you know, the oil in this area has got a fascinating history. You know, the oil industry basically started here and the UNICAL platform, known as Platform A, was named A because it was the first offshore oil platform.

UNOCAL actually started here in Ventura County in Santa Paula after oil was discovered during the Lincoln administration by Lincoln's chief geologist at a place called Sulphur Mountain. And UNICAL's first major office is actually in Santa Paula to this day and they've turned it into an oil field museum, which is a really interesting piece of history they've captured there. As oil began to be developed in this area, petrochemical industry started to advance.

It had a really interesting side effect. We were getting large amounts of oil in those days via the whaling industry. The oil industry kind of stopped the whaling industry.

Even at places like Coho Point up below Point Conception, they had a whale rendering plant up there, you know, near where the Chumash used to be and right next to Western Gate, you know, which is a vital part of Chumash lore, indigenous lore in general. So this was one of the side effects. I want to say benefit.

I don't know that it was a net benefit in the long run, but the whaling industry was killed off by the oil industry. So back to 1969, as I understand it, they tried to stop the seep

with a combination of drilling mud and the metal plates that you mentioned and they never were able to actually cap the leak. It kept going, a couple of oil field engineers told me this, it kept going until pressure ran lower in the reserve and then it gradually began to taper off. And I remember out there in Goleta, we had a heavier oil presence for about, I want to say about seven or eight years.

Empty Wave, Goleta

You know, it's a rough estimate, but I distinctly recall, you know, like I'd walk from Coal Oil Point up to Naples Point, you know, and surf all the other spots north of there on the Gaviota Coast and the whole coast, all the rocks, everything was covered with pitch, asphaltum. And on the cliffs where you see erosion taking place and you can see deep into the coastal morphology, you can see layers of pitch buried in the rock sediment.

And so it was everywhere in 69, but more of it everywhere. Cut to years later, that all kind of disappeared. You know, oil field mining, minerals mining had the effect of lowering the pressure in the reserves and we got less seepage in time rather than more seepage.

And asphaltum is an interesting thing. In the Santa Barbara Channel, you have all these, all this porosity that is exuding methane and asphaltum. And for years, UCSB geology studied it.

Then one day, a team from Woods Hole Oceanographic Institute came out and they were talking to the geology department at UCSB and said, you know, we really want to study oil seepage. And, you know, UCSB geology went, well, have we got something to show you? And they took them out to Coal Oil Point and the geologist from HUI said, wow, we've been looking all over the world for something like this to study.

Their conclusion at the end of study was that approximately, I don't remember the exact number, but it was on the order of multiples of Exxon Valdez spills had come up from

the bottom in that region. For those, you know, listeners that might not know, Exxon Valdez was a 10 million gallon spill. So orders of multitude above that existed there.

And growing up, since I fished, dove, surfed, sailed, did all that stuff, I got really well acquainted with the biome up there. And so, you know, we had a lot of calico bass, halibut, seals, different types of marine life, not a lot of cetaceans compared to what I see up there today. But what was going on is the benthic community, which is the bottom community, starting with the microbial community, was assigning its energy to processing all of the petrochemicals.

Single Fin Style, 1970's, Goleta

And what that did is that left less energy to assign to the rest of the biome to develop. And decades later, I watched a bottom survey that another UCSB student had done a dive survey, and he's swimming over the areas I used to dive, and it looked totally different, Robert. There were fish populations I'd never seen before, bottom fauna I'd never seen before, the whole area was completely transformed.

And there was a lot, lot, lot less asphalt. And at the same time, you'd walk the beach, and that heavy layer of asphalt that was over all the rocks had been minimized, and it was almost like a different place. Cut to the Chumash, you know, who date back thousands of years in the area, and then implementing the use of asphaltum through their entire tribal culture. Caulking the Tomols, coating cooking utensils, all this stuff, the asphaltum was part of their culture.

Cuyahoga River On Fire, 1969

Well, that's how it was when I moved there. It was that pervasive, it was everywhere.

We used to do the same thing that Chumash did, we would use to start fires on the beach, because back then, wetsuits were kind of in their infancy, and coming from a family with six kids, I couldn't really, nor did I really want to wear a dive wetsuit. So we would burn asphaltum on the beach, pitch on the beach to start our fires, and you'd keep a fire burning, you'd start it before you go out in the water, you'd surf until you got frozen, then come in and sit by the fire and warm up, and then go back out and surf some more. But all that changed over the years.

We made fires on the beach illegal, there was less pitch on the beach to burn, and everything really changed, until one day. Here's the one day. We have oil pipelines running all over the region.

We have a couple different refineries, we have pipelines going everywhere, they bring the oil ashore to the processing terminals, and we had a pipeline, the pipeline was worn out, and we had an oil spill at Gaviota, which soiled Gaviota with, I think, a few thousand gallons of oil. And as a result of that, Santa Barbara County said, no, we're not going to let you guys transport oil anymore. And so they stopped oil field activity in the Santa Barbara Channel.

A couple companies went belly up, and I subscribed to the board of supervisors newsletter up there, and I got a note that two kayakers had reported a large oil spill off Goleta Beach, which is just south of Coal Oil Point by about two miles. And we're trying to determine the source, and I wrote them a note back, and I said, well, it's been a few months since we shut down drilling, all of the holding facilities are full, and the pressure is going up in the reserve, and here's where that oil is coming from, based on what the wind has been doing, and what I know of the area. And the next day, t here

was the

Blowout Film, Creative Frontline–Robert Lundahl

funniest bulletin.

We've been informed by an expert resource that it's a naturally occurring seep, and we're probably going to be seeing more of it. So that's how all of that stuff interrelates.

Robert Lundahl

Now you're talking about that particular pipeline that carried oil to the refineries in Kern County, right? Yeah, that's the Bakersfield-Taft area. What was that movie with Robin Williams and Taft? You know, the story about Bakersfield and Taft and their football rivalry?

David Pu'u

Oh yeah.

Robert Lundahl

Anyway, that was very industrialized, and people were pretty hardscrabble and tough. So this wasn't as frou-frou as it is today, with Oprah Winfrey living on the coast and the Prince of Sussex. A lot of people don't know this about California.

You know, they think California is something different.

Robin Williams and Kurt Russell in "The Best of Times," 1986.

David Pu'u

Yeah, I mean, Ventura originally is an oil town and a cow town. When the Graff family moved here, they came from the East Coast, and they landed at Stearns Wharf by schooner. They were hosted by De La Guerra, and the De La Guerra is on coast.

There's a stretch of coast down there that, you know, you guys might do well to farm and ranch. So the McGrath family moved down here, and were one of the first ranches and then farms in Ventura County, along with a couple other people. But that's how, you know, agriculture started here.

And it was very similar the way oil was discovered again during the Lincoln administration, and that attracted workers from back East, from more depressed areas, following, you know, economic Congress. Not unlike what happened during the gold rush.Robert Lundahl

Something happened in the United States of America, politically and socially, as a result of this oil escapade. And also a couple of other events that were negative on the environment, like the day that the Cuyahoga River in Cleveland burst in, well actually it had burst into flames several times. But it finally hit the news that the river was burning, which was a shock.

Goleta Surfer with Oil Rig/Background

There was Life magazine with the oil spill and the urning river, and you know, it was pretty devastating. It was a devastating look at this industrialization post-war.

David Pu'u

I remember that being an incredible shock. What do you mean a river's burning?

Goleta surfer with Oil Rig. Blowout Film, Robert Lundahl

Robert Lundahl

Yeah. Remember that Randy Newman song, burn on big river, burn on?

David Pu'u

Yep. I do.

Robert Lundahl

So this is how we grew up. This is our era. This is what we learned from.

And what America learned from was something oddly different. And it was the result of a senator from Wisconsin that thought that it was probably a good time to take a different course and introduced the first Earth Day. And eventually the EPA was formed shortly thereafter, which contained the first set of laws in the United States to protect the environment and people, and Native people, you know, who live in vulnerable areas and so forth.

So they put the whole package together, you know, to fix these big problems. And it resulted in what we call the National Environmental Protection Act.

There's a red
moon rising On
the Cuyahoga
River
Rolling into Cleveland to the lake

There's a red
moon rising On
the Cuyahoga
River
Rolling into Cleveland to the lake

There's an oil barge
winding Down the
Cuyahoga River Rolling
into Cleveland to the
lake

There's an oil barge
winding Down the
Cuyahoga River Rolling
into Cleveland to the
lake

Cleveland, city of light, city of
magic Cleveland, city of light,
you're calling me Cleveland, even
now I can remember 'Cause the
Cuyahoga River
goes smokin' through my dreams

Burn on, big
river, burn on
Burn on, big
river, burn
onNow the Lord
can make you
tumble Lord can
make you turn
The Lord can make you
overflow But the Lord
can't make you burn

Burn on, big
river, burn on
Burn on, big
river, burn on

"Burn On" Words and Lyrics by Randy Newman

David Pu'u

Yep. A lot of people don't realize that both the EPA and the NOAA were formed as a result of political actions during the Nixon administration. And as I understand it, Nixon had a look at the oil spill in Santa Barbara and was shocked by it.

But he also had a look at all the different departments and agencies tasked with managing all these different aspects of industrial development. And he thought it would be good for the American taxpayer to combine all of these under one organizational umbrella, which was the Environmental Protection Agency at the time. So we centralized all of these entities and it evolved into what it is today.

Same thing with the NOAA.

Robert Lundahl

It has very idealistic language about man and nature living together productively and setting the conditions under which that can take place. I mean, it's really inspiring and progressive, really, you know, for that time. And under Nixon also was created the Clean Air Act and the Clean Water Act separately.

David Pu'u

Right.

Robert Lundahl

So in the era of my youth and perhaps yours, then we all of a sudden had an environmental movement in the country.

Blowout Film, Creative Frontline–Robert Lundahl

David Pu'u

I remember before moving to Santa Barbara, we lived in Whittier, so my dad could commute into his defense work with all the defense contractors. And the air pollution was so bad there in the L.A. Basin. On some days it looked like fog, except it had a brown cast to it.

And I was ill all the time as a child living there. And I used to have to go in every two weeks and get allergy shots, one in each arm. And when we moved out of Whittier and moved up to Santa Barbara, within about three months, I stopped having allergies.

I never had to have another allergy shot. So it said a lot about the role of pollution and air pollution to me about public safety and public health, which really drove the original environmental movement. And today it's far better than it ever was before.

Even in Santa Barbara, I remember as oil companies were being pushed to manage the seeps in the channel. I was at the beach one day and I watched these two barges drop these giant canopies off Coal Oil Point. They're massive.

They're about 100 yards across each. And those canopies sat over some of the methane vents for the oil field. And what they did is they captured the methane and they sent it a few miles north to the Elwood terminal.

That methane was processed and it was used to supply natural gas for Santa Barbara County. The amount of air pollution captured and repurposed as fuel offset all of the exhaust from all the cars in Santa Barbara County. But they finally got a permit to laterally drill and tap that reserve.

And when they did, the production of the two tents went to zero. And what we learned from that is that air pollution in the channel is actually energy resource going to waste. It's high volatile organic compounds going into the atmosphere that can create health problems.

Or you can burn it and use it as fuel. So that's part of where this all heads. You know, it's all about resource management.

Pollution is just a resource out of place. It's putting it in its proper place is a key to building us energy sustainable culture. Which is where I'd like to see it head.

I think probably you would as well, I would imagine. Yeah, you look at regenerative agriculture and it's all based on proper utilization of waste. And that's how you make a rich soil that provides nutrient rich, you know, produce.

Robert Lundahl

It's a transition that's already happening. It's not like, oh what we're going to do about our sustainability transition or our CO2 according to the IPCC and so forth.

Davis Pu'u

You know what happens if we increase CO2 to maybe two and a half, three times what it is today?

Robert Lundahl Plants grow like crazy? **David Pu'u**

Yeah, the dinosaurs come back. And maybe we disappear. I don't know. Bad joke.

Robert Lundahl

Well, it's good to have humor. You know, a lot of people get pretty dire around this climate change, you know, stuff. And that word regenerative is quite interesting.

We've defined regenerative practices that nature likes to take care of itself and grow in according to its own opportunities. And it's quite good at that. And then we say, well, we have to protect nature, right?

We're talking with our indigenous friends and so on about tribal practices. And we use these weird words like, okay, well, that for the non-natives, we want to protect nature, you know, in a way that the native communities have, you know. I guess what that means is taking care of things and appreciating them and understanding how a place like Ash Meadows, which we've discussed, works as a biodiversity hotspot and oasis. They have unique species, 28 endemic species, many endangered species. So this idea of protection, protection versus living there. How do you like to talk about that?

David Pu'u

Well, I think you can go back and look at some of the Chumash history. You know, they were everywhere. You'd find around every waterway, you'd find a village on one side with one tribe and another village on the other side with another tribe. And it was all sustainable until it wasn't. And it became unsustainable for the Chumash at the era that the ranchos began to take over the area. And you began to see a drop in flora and fauna.

I think this is one of the reasons that the Chumash became such an ocean people. They were using the ocean, you know, for a large portion of their food resource. But the population dropped off as the Chumash population dropped off as all these other factors came in.

Then you had missionization, all that stuff. I mean, today we have a real health problem for the public at large because of industrialization of food production. I mean, everybody knows about glyphosate as an endocrine disruptor and how we use it in a lot of factory farm processes.

And it really provides a foundation for disease because you're not meant to be, you know, uptaking an endocrine disruptor in all your foods. And it's cumulative, and it damages everything, which gives rise to the need for medical care where maybe you didn't need it before. Go back to me living in Whittier and having to go see a doctor every two weeks to get injected with an allergen serum, and then moving to a cleaner, better environment where I didn't need that anymore.

So all of this fits together. It all jigsaw puzzles together. And I think where indigenous people have it over contemporary culture, they understand how all these systems work together.

And, you know, they can advise some of these government agencies that are maybe being controlled by agency capture through some of the corporations attached to our political system. They can maybe advise them better. I know my friend Blue Wolf said they're actually recognized as one of the seven sciences in the national forest.

Jane Pauley, NBC News, The Today Show

Robert Lundahl

Native people don't operate on laws created in Washington, D.C. They operate on natural law. And the original instruction set, that's another way it's sometimes described.

David Pu'u

Again, when you talk about indigenous people and indigenous culture, you're creating kind of a generalization. Some people live according to their ancestral tenets. Most do not.

I mean, I look at Hawaii, the poverty level in Hawaii as Hawaiian culture has evolved and gentrification has taken place is incredibly high, Robert. It is really distressing what's happened to the islands. And as that's happened, you've seen a generational drop in net sustainability.

So the problem may be that the Hawaiian people are more American than they are Hawaiian these days. You know, when Hawaii was taken over by a coup, we brought in a completely different system. And the Hawaiian way of life, the indigenous way of life was subverted by a modern manufacturing era of life.

A lot of stuff that Hawaii needs, it all comes in by ship or plane. It all has to be imported. Talk about unsustainable.
You look at the amount of energy a ship uses to get across the ocean or an aircraft uses to get from the East Coast to Hawaii. And that's an incredible resource expenditure. So I think maybe we as indigenous people are part of the problem some of the time.

Robert Lundahl

Yeah, that's fair.

David Pu'u

We've come to rely on these modern systems that we grew up within. I mean, the classic example is my father, you know, growing up in a traditional Hawaiian family, going to war, working for the Department of Defense for the government that actually stole Hawaii from the monarchy. You can't write anything more ridiculous than that.

But that's what happened. That's my family history.

Chapter Five- Battling Goliath

Robert Lundahl

As a filmmaker I spent four years, beginning in July, 2010, investigating the impacts of large solar development on the deserts of my home state of California. Solar development in the deserts of the Southwest was initiated as part of the American Recovery and Reinvestment Act of 2009, which included $6 billion for loan guarantees, an amount that was far exceeded in actuality, over subsequent years.

"Who Are My People?" ©2014 Robert Lundahl

In addition to loan guarantees, the ARRA created a grant program for business. A facility owner could choose to receive a one-time grant equal to 30 percent of the construction and installation costs for the facility. Eligible projects included anaerobic digesters, landfill gas, solar, and wind. With 30% up-front in cash, the business risks of project development were substantially reduced and a "feeding frenzy" ensued. Speculative investors like Goldman Sachs applied for low cost leases on public lands and the queue, to be managed by the Bureau of Land Management, was long, with over 200 projects in Southern California alone.

I had thought of the deserts of Southern California as a grand "backyard" to the polluted environs where I was raised, in Pasadena, Los Angeles County. The deserts

Who Are My People? ©2014 Robert Lundahl

provided "breathing room" for an emerging connected metropolis of Los Angeles, Orange and San Diego Counties, where population had grown exponentially.

With industrial development now threatening the more remote desert regions, I questioned whether and how such large scale development might be managed, and whether there would be anything left of the deserts which had stimulated my curiosity as an adult. The impacts included those to plants and animals, waters, soils and air quality, and to the American Indian cultures I had come to know, making two previous films.

The academic distance I had tried to maintain dissipated when I witnessed the destruction of ancient geoglyphs, giant earth works, made by earlier civilizations, which American Indians attribute to a connection with the Cosmos. These geoglyphs express an intricate set of inter-relationships between places, ancient art, and people, incorporating what scientists refer to as archeo-astronomy. We were destroying the work of their Gallileos in a mad rush to receive the cash grants. Billions were at stake and the world's energy companies were at the door.

The first major project was built, at Ivanpah, and brought on line in 2014. It is a name meaning White Clay Waters, in the Chemehuevi language, in a region known as the best habitat available for the Desert Tortoise, a "Protected Species." 5 square miles were graded. Down the road at another site, the Genesis project had been started. There, Kit Fox were decimated by distemper, a scourge some say was attributed to the urine of construction workers' dogs.

This Place Matters. "Who Are My People?" ©2014 Robert Lundahl

They say the road to hell is paved with good intentions, and while mitigating climate change, or doing our part as a nation is a good intention, it remains an unconvincing argument that remotely sited industrial solar and wind is the answer, given that Germany has added 500 MW of renewable energy a month to their energy "portfolio" using rooftops and parking lots.

There were victories of a sort. A lawsuit had stopped a large facility in Imperial County. And the so called "Largest Solar Project in the World," Blythe Solar, was abandoned in 2011 when opposition exposed poor construction practices and violations as the applicant, Solar Millennium, raced to build infrastructure that would have allowed cash grants to become available. A similar project was mothballed at Rio Mesa in 2013, near beds of Mammoth fossils, and at Hidden Hills in Nevada, where California state anthropologists validated that Paiute cultural lands extended over the project. In a world where we as "civilized peoples" lament the destruction of the "Taliban Buddhas" and ancient Babylon destroyed by war, it is somewhat heartening to know our own American antiquities carry some weight for preservation, though not much. The California Energy Commission indicated 17,000 Indigenous "Sacred Sites" would be destroyed by energy development in the deserts.

After coming to grips with new levels of thoughtlessness and destruction, it was of no particular surprise that the Ivanpah project was revealed in the press in 2014 as "incinerating" the birds of the Pacific Flyway, the migratory pathway followed by hundreds of bird species that converge to the Salton Sea portal south into Mexico, Central and South America. Dead birds included endangered species like the resident Yuma Clapper Rail and iconic ones like Golden Eagles. Projects like Ivanpah have been labelled "Death Traps" because they look like lakes from above. Tired birds navigate down toward rest and water and become "streamers", smoking projectiles hurtling to Earth.

Prayer. "Who Are My People?" ©2014 Robert Lundahl

The Palen project would be the worst. With two enormous towers capped by solar receivers projecting their "brilliance" over the Southeast corner of Joshua Tree National Park, the project had everything going for it. Not only would it destroy Native sacred sites and cultural resources, fry bird species, eliminate many square miles of habitat for plants and animals, it would negatively impact tourism to the National Park and the economic heath of communities like Joshua Tree, at the Park's entrance.

The project was so bad it became one of the few that had been denied a permit by the CEC, California Energy Commission. But then, inexplicably, the applicant, BrightSource, was allowed to amend the application. A renewed project with one tower only and the possible inclusion of a second at a later date, plus an energy storage component to smooth out its power delivery to the grid, was offered conditional approval despite the unmitigable impacts. The project had been denied, then Dracula--like, it had surfaced from the grave and won half-hearted approval.

Numerous Indian tribes had delivered impassioned testimony against the project. Neither was the public happy, according to on-the-record comments. At the darkest hour, it seemed certain a slew of 16 penny framing nails would be hammered into a tiny coffin containing the carcasses of little burned Wrens and Warblers, Tortoise and Kit Fox, and the dreams of Native Americans, long the victims of cultural genocide following California's Gold Rush, and the forced removal of their children to Indian Schools as late as the 1950's.

California's DRECP, or Desert Renewable Energy Conservation Plan, was instituted following the approval of BLM's national plan for the Southwest. The DRECP, a joint effort of federal and state agencies, would allocate 22 million acres to "development " and determine lands also to be "conserved." The DRECP process had been the official channel for receiving the input of "stakeholder groups" including large environmental organizations like the Sierra Club.

It was released publicly in draft form, at a photo op beneath the enormous rotating blades of a giant field of Wind Turbines outside Palm Springs last week. Secretary of the Interior Sally Jewell stood positioned heroically against a dust-blown desert sky. Secretary Jewell joyfully extolled the virtues of renewable energy development in the desert on a scale the world had never known.

74 year old grandmother, Pat Flanagan, is a Board Member of the Morongo Basin Conservation Association. In 1983, she was the field biologist that monitored the prototype Solar One facility at Daggett. Pat had spent the previous weeks rising at dawn, correlating data from thousands of pages of CEC, California Energy Commission and BLM, Bureau of Land Management documents.

She had used a simple search tool across myriads of .pdfs, to track the usage of terminology like "solar receiver" as it applied to the Palen project and its permitting. Oddities emerged. The Palen Project was described by the CEC as being a 750' Tower with a 130 Ft. receiver "atop," yet the BLM docs described a 68 foot "solar receiver." Did "atop" mean "contained within the height of" or "in addition to"?

The CEC and the BLM were not in sync and the language was not clear. As both state and federal agencies were involved, this would seem to invalidate the Palen Project permit. To properly communicate, the BLM draft and the CEC documents would need to be rewritten (reanalyzed) and submitted again to the public for review. If challenged in court, this would become a time consuming process, and time was running out for applicant BrightSource.

Battling Goliath was a disappointment. Goliath was not a very good writer, nor a thorough editor. Goliath couldn't get his facts straight.

As I watched television, I saw President Obama remarkably admit the United States underestimated ISIS forces in Syria, how many people they had, how much money they had, how many towns they had conquered. And I thought, are we so narcissistically absorbed in our own greed that we are failing to see the importance of world events, our treasured antiquities, bird species, or American Indian culture, as we continue to commit an egregious cultural genocide that began in the West in the 1830s?

Pat completed her report. She uploaded it to the CEC website at 9:01 am on Friday the 26th. Then at 3:05 pm, out of the blue, in an action that without doubt shocked the world's energy industries and financial institutions, BrightSource withdrew the project. It was over. Goliath threw in the towel.

The article in the Palm Springs Desert Sun reads: "BrightSource senior vice president Joe Desmond said the developers chose to withdraw their application in part because the project was unlikely to be completed by December 2016, meaning it wouldn't qualify for a 30 percent investment tax credit that expires at the end of that year."
I suppose that is the logical conclusion of a value set that sees life as money and money as life. I expected a better fight. Goliath had wanted it too easy.

Chapter Six- Traditions of the Heart

Shelly Vendiola (Swinomish Tribal Member)

It's loving, caring, and sharing. And that's a thought that was left with us from my uncle Chet Caillou.. And he always spoke about how we need to be loving and caring and sharing with one another, with our guests.

That's who we are. And so those are values. Those are values that hopefully we can pick up and we can pass on to the next generation.

Courtesy Swinomish Tribe

There's a Lushootseed word, it's Hachusidat. And the simplified version of that is education, but really Hachusidat is traditions of the heart. And with traditions of the heart comes compassion.

But tradition of the heart means that we know what our values are and we uphold those values. And it also means that we are informed by nature and the earth around us because that is education. That is our education.

Our wealth is not the almighty dollar. Our wealth is what comes from the sea. That's our wealth.

Our wealth is how we spread the table. Our wealth is how much we can give away. And so it's a real different way of knowing and being than in a Western public school kind of teaching and learning.

Courtesy Swinomish Tribe

And so that is the piece that we would like to bring in and introduce to our neighbors and also have our young people go through these experiences as families, as being connected to our elders and start really picking up that language again. Because many tribes, there are many tribes that are larger that speak pretty fluent or have fluent speakers. We do not have fluent speakers per se, but we have people that are learning to become fluent speakers today.

And so that is why we prioritize that piece. Because I think there's a lot to be learned by these ancient stories and just the terminology, which cannot be confused. It's not the English language.

And terminology is often embedded in that, a value system that really is connected to how we survive on the earth and on the water. And it's thousands of years old. Why? Because our ancestors had that time to study their surroundings.

We're not ever of the ego mindset that says that we are in a hierarchy manner. We are in an existence where one is above another. That never existed because we had to work together to survive circumstances where we didn't have electricity and we didn't have cars.

And it was pretty difficult actually for our ancestors to live, hence studying the earth so that they could survive on. And we're soon to be coming to that because we see what happened in Texas when the grid went down and we're seeing a lot of fires and people are having a hard time breathing. And so I'm just saying that when we learn to survive on the earth in a traditional manner, perhaps we can thrive because the earth can take care of herself.

Swinomish Racing Canoes, Courtesy Swinomish Tribe

There's been ancient civilizations that we know about that there's evidence that had pretty sophisticated technology. I would have to say that I feel like our technology is pretty sophisticated today. I could be wrong, but here we are again.

It's not like we haven't been down this road as many scientists and many archeologists and many people who have evidence who've studied the earth can attest to. And that's something that I think we have these ancient stories and embedded in their stories are some of these things that we feel like are so way beyond us. And part of that is intuition.

The other part of it is how we do well in our environment. So when we say living in a traditional manner, what I'm saying is we have a canoe practice. And in that practice, we have racing canoes and then we have journey canoes.

The journey canoes are much bigger. The racing canoes are slimmer, slicker, lighter, and faster. We have that technology still today.

We have that knowledge. We have one longhouse in the center of our village. And the thing about longhouses is if you think about how those were built before colonization happened, before the 1800s, everybody had to participate.

Trditional Coast Salish Longhouse, Courtesy ICT

Because if you think about the wood and the logs and felling the tree and many trees to build a longhouse that is massive or over 100 people can live, that's a lot of heavy lifting. And so not one person or five people. It was a community of people that worked together to put up a longhouse that people could live in during the winter, that they could have a place to weave.

They had a place to tell stories. They had a place to be worn in. And so it's actually very practical.

It's very practical living off the land. And if we have that mentality, I think perhaps a lot of people will be able to thrive in a healthier way given the circumstances that we're in today. And I must say that I'm really, really excited that a lot of the women are coming forward in indigenous communities. And their voices are being amplified now because of that connection that we as women have to the earth. That we birth children. We are reflections of the earth herself. We feed our children. So a lot of those kind of teachings are coming back as well. Midwifery, for example.

All of the homeopathic medicine that's happening today. Ancient, ancient. If you think about where did that come from, it's old. Thousands of years old. And then we have the Western medical field. But I'm just saying that there is ancient knowledge that we can pick up and we can learn from.

Like I like to practice yoga and I like to meditate. I like to do qigong, which is ancient. Why? Because it helps me to de-stress. So I'm picking up things that are helpful. That's not to say that you have to do one thing one way all the time. Because that's sort of impractical given the ever-changing environment that we live in.

Carrie and Mary Dann, Western Shoshone, Wikipedia

Because the environment is always changing. Just like as we age, we as human beings,
we change. We are reflections of the earth.

And so therefore, a long time ago, Carrie Dann of Western Shoshone, her and her sister ran the Dann Ranch. And they had a big strife with the federal government trying to take away their cattle and not let them be who they were. She always said, back in the 90s, she always said, the earth has a fever.

The earth has a fever and she's going to purge because that's what you do when you have a fever. It's a no-brainer. We are of the same DNA.

That's what John Trudell always says. We are of the same DNA of the earth. So we have to behave as if the earth matters.

John Trudell, Courtesy PBS, Independent Lens

And so that's a large part of the work that we are trying to do in our Protect Mother Earth subcommittee and this resilience project. And so my hope and my prayer is that it will be meaningful for our community and those that are partners to us and beyond. So we're just doing the best we can.

That's all. We're just doing the best we can to remember who we are and practice who we are. For those who don't know, the Swinomish tribe is part of a larger community of Salish peoples.

And across this world, I call it the Coast Salish universe, there's been a lot of trouble and strife. And part of that has been flooding, actual flooding of villages and so forth, like we've seen in Alaska. And there's been political challenges around that.

Robert Lundahl, Filmmaker, Journalist

Can you talk a little bit about what some other tribes and villages are seeing and what hardships they're facing that are actual and physical on the ground due to climate change?

Shelly Vendiola

Yeah. So we have what's called the National Congress of American Indians, and it's a pretty big lobbying force of all of the indigenous communities throughout the country. And Fawn Sharp is the president, and she is also a Quinault tribal member.

And the tribes on the coast, where her tribe is on the west coast, are being inundated by flooding. And there's a lot of storm surges happening, tsunami type situations that are occurring, and the land is really eroding. And so they're being forced, the whole tribe, there's little tribes near Quinault.
Taholah village Quinault Tribe

And those tribes are looking at plans to relocate because of the way that the tides are sort of blowing into the land and how the land is then eroding, kind of like the Gwich'in and the people up in the north on the Arctic. That their land is being impacted as well. It's eroding, it's going into the sea, and the caribou are going away.

Taholah, Quinault Village

They're being impacted. Same with our salmon. So it's the ecosystems that we're all connected to by the earth and the water.

And the salmon swim all the way up there and come all the way back down, up north and come all the way back down. And so if they're not making it, it impacts a lot of

Fish Farming, Greece

indigenous communities. And so we're seeing a lot of what's happening in British Columbia with the, there's some fish farm operations that still want to operate.

So there's blockades going on up there because what happens when those kind of fish escape is they intermingle with the wild salmon. But some people call those farm salmon frankenfish. And there was a lot more of them back in the 90s, but as our fishery folks here, commercial fishery folks, non-native fisheries and native fisheries alike started to see the impact of that wild salmon.

The fact that they could make the flesh of that salmon any color by injecting dye to make it look real healthy and pink, as opposed to what it would look like, grayish, kind of whitish flesh, not very appetizing. And then they started having a lot of fecal matter, like smothering the below the sea. And so it started to kill off all the sea life.

And then there's sea lice, you know, on and on. So when that happens, your whole ecosystem is impacted. And so there's been a big movement to shut down those fish farms around here.

We had started trying to get all that farm salmon out of the water because what it does is it intermingles, like I said, and then you have another kind of species, I guess. So those are the kind of impacts that we're seeing, as well as, you know, the Burrard Swelltooth Nation up there in British Columbia.

They're very concerned about their waterway. And it's very, very slim channel that these big oil tankers and other cargo ships go through. And there's a lot of ships that
go through there. And it's really impacting their sea life and their ability to practice who they are. And so they're protesting up there. And on top of that, they have that Trans Mountain Pipeline coming through.

And it's not unlike what we're seeing on the Mississippi. But that pipeline happens to have oil that would feed into the reservation's stolen land, which is called March Point, where two oil refineries are located on the north end of our reservation. And how
that happened wasn't by agreement by the tribe, of course.

At that time, Ulysses Grant signed a proclamation, well, it was an executive order that said that, oh, this is really the, he demarked a map of the reservation and he cut off March Point, that tip that goes way out into the bay. And he claimed that that was not reservation land. And now today, you know, industry has been built on there.

There's two oil refineries that have been on there for a while. And our shellfish is poisoned out there. So we know that not to go gather shellfish out there. And so that's the circumstances. It's just on and on. I can go on, I'll give you a lot of different examples.

But that is the reality that we're faced with. That's why we have to educate one another, we're together, because it's not just impacting us anymore. That refinery is not just impacting us anymore. There's going to be like, what, more oil tankers coming through? Not a good idea. Tribes around here don't think that's a good idea. Well, the word on the street about the oil industry is where there is oil, there will be spills.

I mean, that came up at Standing Rock and with Dakota Access Pipeline and Keystone XL and Trans Mountain. And the protests that are occurring in British Columbia at Wet'suwet'en to block, you know, the pipeline. So there's a major effort going on, you know, politically and culturally, that's in the news.

Robert Lundahl

And I can't believe Facebook, you know, how many people are committed and working and protesting. It seems like a large movement. Does that surprise you that suddenly there's this presence of the care and concern you're talking about in a real world circumstance?

Shelly Vendiola

That's quite difficult, you know, as far as negotiating with these companies, or the regional, territorial, provincial governments, state governments. It's hopeful. It's hopeful. I'm hoping now with that surge that things can change, really.

I'm of the mindset that if we don't stop things now and change our behavior, and some people will say, well, we're so addicted to oil, that can never happen, that we have to take our time. But we already know that the earth will continue heating, and the more we develop fossil fuel industry and use that addiction, then we are pretty much sitting ducks. And I really feel that there's a lot of sweet deals that are being made, a lot of things that sound green and good and renewable.

But I feel like the earth should have rights, and that this next generation are exerting their rights by suing the state, for example, brave young souls that are suing the state. And of course, there's a lot of legal beagles that are supporting that work as well. And so that is promising.

When we have legal entities that are willing to defend the earth, and I'm talking about, it comes from that book, Earth Jurisprudence, but I'm also talking about those lobbying, environmental legal lobbying groups that are really fighting hard to litigate matters of wrongdoing. And so that's the more extreme than mediating and developing strategies for mitigation. It's really a win-lose situation.

And I really feel that the fossil fuel industry has put us there. We're in a win-lose situation, and we can take our time and let the earth continue to warm and hope and pray, or we can stop our behavior like we did with this coronavirus. I think that virus had a lot to teach us about how we might be able to adapt better and more emergent.

Climate Change is Here: The Movie, by Robert Lundahl,

But I don't know, like there's a lot of naysayers still who didn't believe that the virus even exists. Just like there's a lot of people that want to say that there is not a climate crisis,

but I like what Gore was saying in Inconvenient Truth. It's certainly inconvenient for a lot of people that don't want to look at it, but we need more people to be brave enough to look at it and to actually do something rather than sit on the fence and wait for someone else to do it, because it's only our future at stake.

Buddhist Teacher and Anthropologist Joan Halifax with Thomas Banyaca (Hopi)

So I'm of the mindset that it is a crisis, and we have to stop bad behavior now, and we have to start mitigating in a clear and coherent manner so that we can all survive.
Thomas Banyaka talked about this many years ago, the Hopi Survival Kit. That's what that book is.

We read that. There's some knowledge in there. Well, it's pretty amazing to be alive in these days because we have all these things that are going on, like the protests and the reclamation of language and identity and relationship to the land and those kinds of things and the public protests, but at the same time, just down the road, you have 121 degree temperatures in British Columbia and whole towns bursting into flame.

Yep. And the relationships seem to be expressible scientifically in terms of probability and temperature rise and things like that, that it isn't a direct line, but there's a circumstantial relationship. I'm just hoping that tribes aren't divided by what would be the best strategy moving forward.

My hope and my prayer is that we, as the indicator species, will take action for the benefit of not only the future, but those indigenous people that are south of us that are being impacted now because of our convenient ability to drive a car or fly a plane or transport something because it's costing them their lives and their livelihood now, today. Massive communities have been impacted by the oil industry. Look at Nigeria.

So, in Nigeria, one of the elders shared the story that it's changed their way of life, and how it's changed their way of life is that they used to be able to go around in these villages as a way of resolving conflict. They used to be able to go around and knock at the door and sing these ancient songs by way of spotlighting a wrongdoing and going to that person that did the wrongdoing to their relatives' homes and doing this. And that was a peacemaking process.

But when they built those huge Shell oil operations there next to these villages, if you see any kind of oil refinery, you'll see that they have lights on 24-7. They never go off. And so, to them, in Nigeria, it was like it was daylight all the time.

Shell Oil Refinery, Ogoniland, Nigeria

It's like when you live in Alaska and it stays daylight all the time. It was like that. So, that ritual and that way of knowing and being, in terms of your values around how you treat a wrongdoing, that was no longer.

They couldn't do that because it never got dark. It had to be in the cloak of darkness. And so, it changes a way of life because when you can't go in the cloak of darkness and practice a ritual around a wrongdoing and have some kind of resolve by that person's family, then you are having to modify a way of life and that dispute resolution strategy goes away. You have to do something else. And so, it changes a culture's behavior and it changes the culture's food source even when you have these kinds of things happening. And here we are in the land of the privileged and we can take our time maybe and we can wait and see what's right. But while Indigenous people in another continent or south of us or even north on the Arctic are being impacted now, their livelihoods, their homelands are going in the water. So, I'm of the mindset that we have to change our behavior now and we have to lock arms together and stop pretending like we can't do it.

"They were ready to take the oil, and we told them they would no longer take the oil. Even in Dere, they packed up and left," Karalole, a member of the Federation of Ogoni Women's Association (FOWA), proudly declared as she recounted the nonviolent demonstration she along with other Ogoni people of the Southern Nigerian ethnic group participated in that ultimately led Shell Oil to abandon their drilling site in their land."

Ms Magazine

Robert Lundahl, Filmmaker, Journalist

Well, activists were killed in Nigeria, right? Ken Saro-Wiwa. And about that time, I was reading also about Ecuador and the Ashuar people and the Waorani people and how their lands had been polluted with oil and that rivers had been polluted and so forth. And those were places for sustenance and food supply and community well-being. And there's a certain amount of that in Alaska, but there's a number of problems in Alaska in the villages. And one of them is sewage. There's no sewage system.

Rust Fungus, Kivalina, Alaska

There's no pollution control sometimes, or if pollution is released into a river or stream, it's not necessarily addressed. It can be mitigated in other ways rather than say stopped or removed or those kinds of things. And so from the research, it's been appalling to me how the conditions seem to be deteriorating in the Bering Sea villages and traditional hunting and fishing get more difficult.

The ice pack is melting. The ice pack protects the shoreline from erosion and destruction. And the permafrost, our industrial facilities, even the oil facilities are leaning and falling over and breaking and spilling oil and these kinds of things.

And so it seems like that's another part of the crisis, but from a human rights perspective, it's appalling.

Shelly Vendiola

Well, there's this other movement happening today, and it's really heartening that young people are taking to the streets and there is this resurgence of movement happening.
Standing Rock being one of the drivers, I think, to show people that, hey, we can do this. You can come and help. It's going to be hard perhaps, but standing together, we're stronger in numbers. And the fact of the matter is that that's how change happens over time.

Martin Luther King and all of the marches and protests he did, and then Billy Frank Jr. and all the fishing wars that were happening. It's just another iteration. And what's causing alarm, I think, is because of the fires and is because people are talking
about the salmon going away and people are getting educated.

And here in the state of Washington, some schools are actually trying their best to partner with tribes and find out what the issues are and find out how can we have you come and speak in our science class, or how can we have you come and talk to our young people about this climate issue or the cultural ways of knowing and being and how we should behave in the world. And it's with that kind of energy, it's with that kind of education that we can pull together. We are also lifting on a term that comes from a story of pushing up the sky, and the term is yahout.

In the Lushootseed, it's *yahout*. And *yahout* means to lift together. And so we're bringing those kind of words out in our language to show the way forward because that story that comes with that word, where that word is highlighted, is about people who are different and speak different languages walking around in a world where the sky was too low and bumping their heads on it.

But they had no way to communicate with one another because they all spoke different languages. But then one day, one of the elders came and said in the elders council, they called to seek advice on what to do. So we'll have a word.

It'll be *yahout*, to proceed forward together. We'll say that word at a certain time, at a certain place, and we'll all lift together our shaved poles from those long time ago. These used to be really tall trees.

We'll shave them into poles and then we'll lift together. And that's that *yahout*. And that's kind of example of a story I was talking about earlier, where there's a lot of wisdom there.

And you don't have to overthink it. It's pretty practical, pretty practical, how we survive on the earth together. And that's what we're hoping to teach the young generation now.

Like how to pick some of that knowledge up, because they're going to have to work together. It's beyond our tribe's means to mitigate this situation, quite honestly. We don't have a choice.

Chapter Seven- The Importance of Simple Things Robert Lundahl

"There are known knowns; there are things we know we know. We also know there are known unknowns; that is to say we know there are some things we do not know. But there are also unknown unknowns -- the ones we don't know we don't know. And if one looks throughout the history of our country and other free countries, it is the latter category that tend to be the difficult ones."

-Secretary of Defense Donald Rumsfeld, 2002

Spirit Runners, Mojave National Preserve

The matter of the construction of large scale industrial solar and wind renewables has been of concern to me since 2010. At that time I embarked on what would become a filmmaker's life-journey, documenting a massive scale industrial development agenda, justified by "The War on Climate Change," that played out across the deserts of Southern California.

The justification for siting over 200 industrial facilities across this remote region, characterized by pristine ecosystems and thousands of years of American Indian culture and antiquities seemed specious, as Germany added 500 MW a month of renewable energy on rooftops and parking lots, close to where it would be used.

Through following a series of proposed industrial solar projects, and documenting opposition to them -- I came to learn new lessons in the importance of simple things.

It was humbling to film and describe the federal government's approach to this mega-scale solar industry land development. Public land was leased at bargain rates to project developers from a variety of countries. Project budgets would run up to 2 billion dollars and developers stood in line to receive 30% "up-front" cash grants.
The level of complexity was staggering, as was the potential financial reward for industry. The opportunity to stimulate the economic resources of communities through support of local rooftop solar was avoided, while American Indian antiquities were bulldozed.

The pro-large solar argument had been made by the California Energy Commission, as early as Summer, 2010. The California Renewable Portfolio Standard (RPS) is one of the most ambitious renewable energy standards in the country. The RPS program requires investor-owned utilities, electric service providers, and community choice aggregators to increase procurement from eligible

renewable energy resources to 33% of total procurement by 2020. In response, decisions would be guided by "OverridingConsiderations" the perceived necessities involved in meeting the RPS standard. Local economy, conservation and culture would take a back seat.

As individuals we may express a preference that the last stands of rare plants like the Crucifixion Thorn not be removed from the planet, or that large solar "Power Towers" like those at Ivanpah, the first utility scale mega-solar installation not incinerate birds migrating along the Pacific Flyway, or that thousands of protected

Desert Tortoise not have their burrows graded, their young (and eggs) obliterated, and adults' habitat removed forever.

We may prefer, politically, that the American "boom and bust" cycles of Western development, be avoided in favor of the slow and steady persistence of communities, hanging on to life in a parched landscape of mysteries and spiritual connection to the land itself.

But the CEC had their marching orders in light of the RPS. Most Americans, rightly and wrongly, assume that amid calls for sacrifice, whether in actual war, or in the so called "Great War on Climate Change," things get a little off-track. But as Rumsfeld states in the famous quotation above, we don't know what we don't know.

Seen from above, the topography of Southern California is a "Basin and Range" landscape of mostly north-south parallel mountain ranges. Major ranges to the west like the San Gabriel, San Bernardino and San Jacinto Mountains are upthrust from the San Andreas Fault. The Garlock Fault forms the Tehachipis, to the northwest. These mountains are the divide between the semi-arid coastal plain and the Mojave Desert. These ranges block incoming storms from the Pacific, forming "rain shadows," where descending warm air creates desert conditions.

Pat Flanagan, desert conservationist and board member of the local Morongo Basin Conservation Association, was the field biologist monitoring birds at the prototype
[4]
Solar One facility at Daggett, in 1983. Today, still surveying the ground, she sees sand–wind blown (aeolian) sand, remnant from a vast array of interior lakes, whose drying began in the late Pleistocene Epoch with the end of the last Ice Age. So called Aeolian Sand, remnant from a vast array of interior lakes, whose drying began in the late Pleistocene Era, transverse the Mojave.

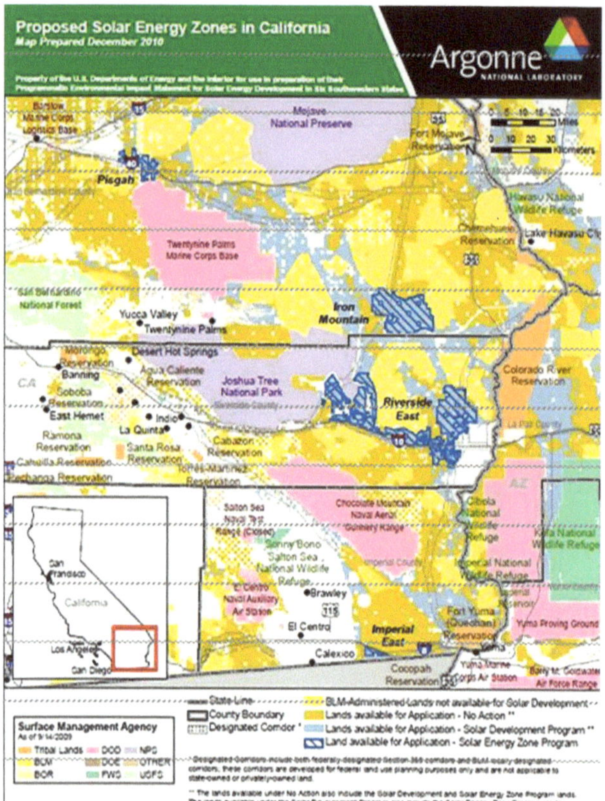

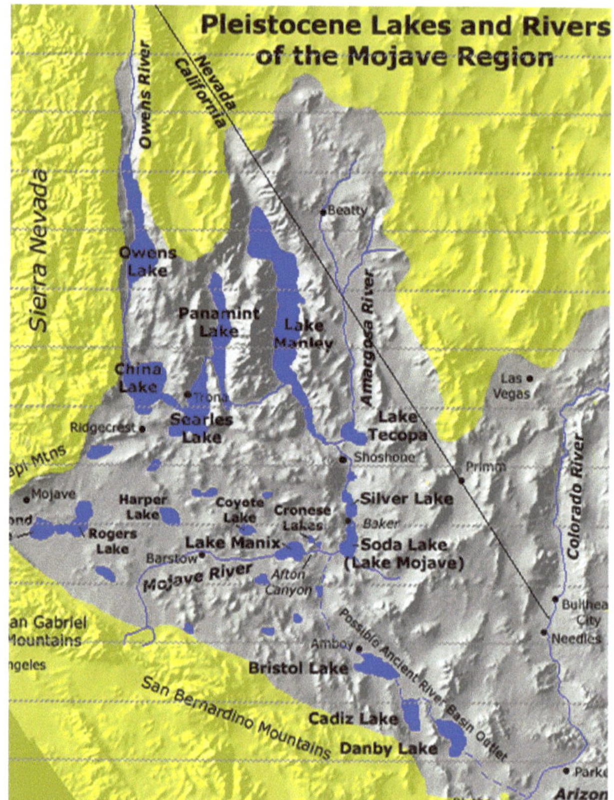

both a dangerously faux landscape and a new demand for water where none exists today.

In fact, the sand dunes, and sand sheets, unique features in the Mojave Desert ensure the 22 million acres described by the Desert Renewable Energy Conservation Plan for the siting of large solar projects, is on the world's research map, along with the Sahara, as a world class sand transport laboratory.

Some large scale solar projects are to be put in the Silurian Valley, a magnificently beautiful landscape of purple mountains and unspoiled vistas, and others are to be located in and around Tecopa, a resort and spa area. While this may seem inconsistent from the standpoint

of conservation values, it is desirable for companies to locate solar fields on slopes of less than 5%, to have maximum control over the positioning of arrays. This most often means locating them at low or negative altitudes on sand deposits and transport areas. The criteria by which projects are to be sited thus follow construction prerogatives.

The USGS, United States Geological Survey, writes:

About 48% of the entire area is less than 5% slope, and 8.3% is less than 1% slope, the favored slope category, deposits underlying the entire area are either mixed eolian-alluvial origin, or are fine grained alluvial deposits, and thus are susceptible to eolian dust and sand transport, especially after disturbance. In addition, in this slope category, 89% of the area is susceptible to flooding based on the age and geomorphology of alluvial deposits. These maps are examples of several we present for decision-making with respect to hazards and ecological attributes in the face of climate change.

Photo Caption: Airborne dust from grading private land outside Blythe, California, rises from the desert floor. On desert pavement, a monolayer of pebbles overlies a stone-poor to stone-free matrix of silt, clay and fine sand, derived principally from wind-blown dust. When grading takes place, the desert pavement is scraped away leaving powdery soils, which become airborne, creating Dust-Bowl like conditions. Photo: Lundahl.

The Silurian Valley, in particular, demonstrates the myriad problems created from a focus on slope as a single determining factor for project siting. 17,000 acres in the Silurian have been proposed for the eventual development of solar and wind. The Silurian Valley is the end drainage for the Mojave River, which sources in the San Bernardino Mountains, and snakes east and north toward Death Valley. The valley is one of the most dramatic examples of a "sand transport area." Enormous sand sheets bury mountains to the east, driven by westerly winds. The area is a wildlife corridor between two National Parks, Death Valley and the Mojave National Preserve. It is also an avian migration corridor. And, the area is along the auto route from Palm Springs to Death Valley, one of the top destinations for Canadian, French and German tourists, who come for unspoiled vistas.

A study of 77 soil types in the Mojave River Area, San Bernardino County, by the USDA Soil Conservation Service finds that as the as the river descends into basins, taking into account degree of slope, water erosion, and root depth, 31 have a "high hazard" of soil blowing, and 13 demonstrate a "moderate hazard". These soil types include Bryman loamy fine sand, Cajon sand, Cajon-Wasco, cool, complex, and Lovelace loamy sand.

Dust Storm, Texas, 1935

It is sand, that very simple and obvious fact of the desert, that the federal government has seemed to ignore in the DRECP.

Although large scale projects have been proposed at sand transport locations such as Ford Dry Lake (Genesis) exposing them to disastrous flooding in 2013, even claiming the lives of two company representatives downed in an observation plane surveying the damage, this kind of impact was perceived as disconnected from the whole.

The realization that there is sand in the desert, continually moving, blowing, flowing, relocating in a vast transport system dating back thousands of years and inhibiting construction activities seems to have escaped policy makers and applicants alike. Plants hold sand in place, along with mycorrhizal fungi associated with those desert plants. When plants are removed, ancient sands begin to travel.Large solar projects spread across multiple square miles, whose permitting requires water for construction, mirror washing and other activities, may have significantly underrepresented required water usage. Joshua Tree's Cascade Solar project, at Coyote Dry Lake, requires ten times the water estimated to tamp down and manage sand and silt at the project, particularly during construction, but also during times when the wind is up. Original estimates of .07 acre/feet usage per acre expanded to actual usages of .7 acre/feet per acre.

Sparrow. Lake effect, Cascade Solar, Coyote Dry Lake. Photo: Deborah Bollinger.

Where will the water come from in an arid region that is potentially growing even more arid?

The larger question looms: In light of required grading and soils disturbance on such a massive scale, blowing silt threatens to turn a land of ancient soils and delicate ecosystems into an unmanageable "dust-bowl," an unusable and unstable sacrifice zone of previously unseen proportions.

Whereas the dustbowl areas of the Great Depression throughout the Midwest were able to remediate themselves by virtue of access to water from many rivers and streams, the same may not be said for the Mojave Desert.

The importance of simple things, and their ignorance, may unleash unintended and cascading consequences.

Overburdened state and federal agencies, under pressure to lease land and permit hundreds of large solar projects across an area the size of Delaware, have overlooked the obvious "beneath their feet."

Perhaps that is because their feet are not in the Mojave, nor are they in Southern California, but in Washington DC, and Sacramento, and other densely inhabited cities where the Earth beneath their feet is covered with concrete and asphalt.

As Donald Rumsfeld so stated, the unknown unknowns are the difficult ones.
*Over 200 are proposed and with many approaching 8000 acres, that equals 2500 square miles, a potential land area larger than the state of Delaware.

Pat Flanagan points out, it is not only about sand, but water. California has experienced an epic drought of four years duration. The drought has been caused by a resilient high pressure system pushing Pacific Storms far to the North. While researchers indicate there appears to be no direct link to climate change, Marty Hoerling, co-editor of a climate report published in the Bulletin of the American Meteorological Society, and a research meteorologist with the National Oceanic and Atmospheric Administration, noted that high-pressure systems have increased everywhere. While climate change makes extreme weather events like the

California drought ten times more likely, natural variability plays a much larger role. Comparing the periods of 1871-1970 with 1980-2013, the authors wrote that there was "no appreciable long-term change in the risk for dry climate extremes over California since the late 19th century." California has always been prone to drought, as long term residents like Flanagan appreciate. It is especially a fact of life amid the Mojave's varied "Basin and Range" topography, a fact of life that state and federal entities overlook.

Chapter Eight– The 100' Wave David Pu'u

Robert Lundahl, Filmmaker, Journalist

I'm here today with David Pu'u and David it's really good to see you and we're going to talk about an area of the coast that's very near and dear to my heart because I grew up like you as a surfer in California and I live very close to Morro Bay.

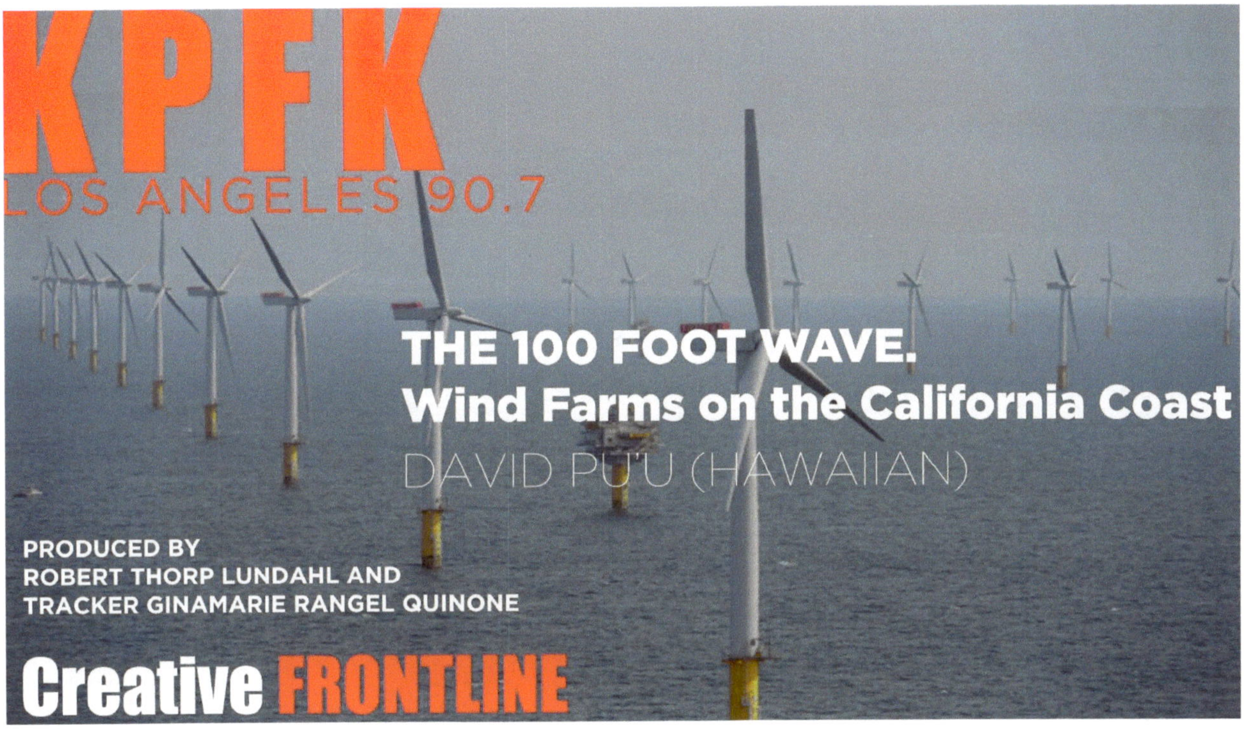

Now we're going to talk about Morro Bay which has for a long time been a remote beautiful area that has been sort of off the map you know to development and now we're seeing something different take place. So can you give me a little bit of background of this giant wind farm that's being planned for the central coast of California and you know I heard something like 20 to 60 miles offshore and 900 foot towers.

What do you know about it?

David Pu'u

Well initially I first heard about it in a meeting here with the state and with Bureau of Ocean Energy Management here in Ventura and I went there with one of my buddies Blue Wolf who's a Barbarino Chumash and a marine biologist and we sat in on the meeting and they were talking about managing the Channel Islands and oh by the way we're thinking about putting wind farms in there and possibly other places on the coast and the representative from Bureau of Ocean Energy Management told us in the course of the meeting that they would never permit that. So here we are years later and we are seeing these projects begin to move forward.

Robert Lundahl, Filmmaker, Journalist

So this is an area of pristine coves and beaches and sea life and how would you describe it?

David Pu'u

Well it's pretty vital I mean it's upstream of the Santa Barbara Channel which historically has got a lot of oil deposits within the channel. I think when Juan Cabrillo first sailed down the channel when he's exploring the coast his navigator documented the oil seepages in the Santa Barbara Channel and said the ocean was black for miles and the fumes were so strong the people on the ship thought they might be overcome. Well central coast doesn't have those oil deposits and so it's a pretty clean region environmentally.

It doesn't have the petrochemical effluent to deal with. So yeah it's a beautiful place to go with pretty vital ecosystems. It doesn't have a large coastal population base or near coastal population base until you get to Paso Robles inland there's a bit more people.

So you don't have a really damaged you know or threatened watershed putting effluent into the ocean there. So it's a pretty pristine area as a result.

Robert Lundahl

Well that's really interesting and it points out the beginning of some of the issues concerns and problems. So one of the things that's brought up has been brought up has been this corridor, power corridor actually for cabling to all these wind farms that would attach somewhere in Morro Bay, Morro Bay Harbor. They have other development plan for Morro Bay Harbor like a lithium battery factory that's huge that's being planned there.

So there's a systemic development and I don't know how integrated it is but it's pretty big and the cabling that goes out to sea to all of these 900 foot towers is a special corridor that's been allotted or allowed in the Chumash National Marine Sanctuary proposal. So can you talk a little bit about the origins of the Chumash Marine

Sanctuary? I understand that it's being put forward by the Northern Chumash Tribal Council which is a non-profit not a tribe.

So how did all that come about?

Morro Rock

David Pu'u

Well, it actually was motivated through Surfrider (Foundation) Sam Lewis, who was pushing for it. They wanted to get a Chumash organization to bless the effort. So they partnered up with the Northern Chumash Council which actually is not affiliated with the reservation or any actual Chumash tribe.

They're not intrinsically Chumash at all but they have the name and they're an NGO. So they're 501c3 with tax exempt status. So they married up with the Northern Chumash Council and they kept petitioning NOAA to do this.

I've been to a couple meetings with Blue Wolf who's a Barbarino Chumash with people in Morro Bay, the fishermen, some of the local business people, and Blue Wolf's position as you know a coastal Native is that the reservation never agreed to do this. They're not interested in doing this and most of the Native Chumash tribes have not agreed to do this. It's only the Northern Chumash Council which isn't Chumash.

So you know that's how that all happened.

Robert Lundahl, Filmmaker, Journalist

And you mentioned the role of NOAA and as you know I've been working on renewable energy development, deployment issues in the desert regarding solar. And you had mentioned that NOAA had a heavy hand on this, as an agenda, as an industry, as a government agency agenda. So can you explain that?

David Pu'u

Well NOAA has their marine sanctuary program, which is global in scope. It's tied to agendas categorized under the UN sustainable development program. And so all of these agencies sister together under the UN's various agendas.

There's Agenda 21 which is now transferred to Agenda 2030. And all of these sustainability and control programs are located there. So the UN has embedded itself in all these different agencies including NOAA.

And NOAA manages the funding to all its subsidiary entities. Like one thing I don't think many people are even aware of is that the Coast Guard manages the Seaman Buoy System. Seaman buoys are telemetry devices that measure marine conditions out at sea.

And the Coast Guard is tasked with managing them. But NOAA manages the funding for the Coast Guard to maintain the buoys. Now the buoys constantly need maintenance because they're in a relatively severe environment.

Ocean salinity and alkalinity being what it is, electronics fail. So sometimes NOAA just does not pay the Coast Guard to go do their job. And you lose your eyes.

Those buoys are principal aids to navigation and they go down. So this goes to how these agencies are tasked with disseminating taxpayer funds.

Robert Lundahl, Filmmaker, Journalist

Got it. Well you said that their process is not necessarily public.

David Pu'u

No, I've been to quite a few meetings as I guess you call them, a stakeholder. I work as a weather and logistics analyst for a company called K38 Rescue which is a marine training company tasked with doing risk study and mitigation and disaster response and training agencies in rescue response in the water using PWC systems, you know, jet ski based systems. So we have had to go to a lot of these meetings.

And when I say me, we, I mean myself, the woman I work for who runs K38 Rescue who's Shawn Alladio, and some of our other affiliates within the organization. And we noticed that what the agencies tend to do is they will be under their mandate which gone from the UN into whatever agency is doing the program. And by the time they get around to public commentary, they have what's called a '"stakeholder meeting."

K38 Rescue for California Law Enforcement

But it's at that point where they've actually decided what they're going to do. And the stakeholder meeting is more of a formality than anything else. I mean, I have an ongoing joke where the stakeholder meeting is kind of like the stake through the vampire's heart.

They use us as members of the public or subject matter experts to hold their stake and then we're done and they go on and do what they're going to do. And this is just, you know, it's just what they do. You know, sometimes that's good.

Sometimes it's not so good. What results?

Robert Lundahl, Filmmaker, Journalist

Well, as we talked, I was reading and listening to a podcast from Julie Carte of the Los Angeles Times and she's a wonderful writer and was talking a lot about the impacts to the community and the perception in the community and what people want. And you had mentioned the interest of the Barbarino Chumash tribe, which is a federally recognized tribe. And where do they come down on all this?

David Pu'u

Well, Marcus Lopez is chairman of the Barbarinos. Blue Wolf works with Marcus and some of the other Chumash. And their whole position is, as an ocean based tribe, is the commons are not to be sequestered from use by any of the indigenous people or the American public.

They're owned in common by all mankind. And so what NOAA is doing with some of these programs is actually fencing the area off so they can manage it. Now, the problem with management is they're not subject matter experts in particular.

Some of them aren't even connected to the ocean, but they're making rules for the fishermen, the public, ocean going people, ocean tribes, who the ocean isn't an asset to them.

It's for a lot of us, especially, you know, for some of the indigenous people, we look at the ocean as being our home. You know, my colleague in Hawaii, Pahaku, says that he has a quote that I'd like to repeat.

The ocean is our home. Land is where we go to rest. And it's really how we view it. We

view it as our home. So it's very personal to us.

Robert Lundahl

You mentioned a burial that you discussed as being present in a residential area, a very high value residential area of Santa Barbara County. Can you talk about the connections between your culture, the indigenous Hawaiian culture, and the Chumash culture, and how you and your colleague, your Chumash colleague, responded to this burial and showed your respect and so on?

David Pu'u

Well, it's an archaeological sensitive site located in Montecito, shoreward of a surf break called Hammond's Reef. That area is in the middle of a lot of high-end real estate development. Land in Montecito is heavily regulated and developments often exceed tens of millions of dollars per unit.

Initially, a developer had decided he was going to close off a grandfathered beach access way that led from a small residential development down through this open meadow, which was then known as Hammond's Meadow, that surfers used to access the wave there at Hammond's Reef. As Surfrider Foundation was just getting started,

they caught wind of this and Surfrider's original mandate was to maintain ocean access for the public and prevent the walling off of the ocean from the public. So they took the task and Mark Massara and Tom Pratt, who was another litigator that was one of the original Surfrider Foundation members, litigated and were able to keep that access open, and they weren't able to develop this last stretch of coastal land there.

In process, we learned that it was actually an archaeologically sensitive Chumash burial site. The Chumash call it Shalawa, and that area has been under threat by a variety of different actors over the years, and the Barbareño and the Chumash are trying to preserve it.

Robert Lundahl

Like going way, way back. How did they get here? Where did they come from? Who

are these people, these Chumash people?

Illustration, Chumash Village

David Pu'u

Well, it's really funny. Blue Wolf did his genetics, and he's actually got Mongolian DNA. A lot of the people that we know as Chumash today arose as a result of the missionization process in California.

The Catholic Church and the Spaniards brought up prisoners from Mexico to breed with the Chumash to dilute the tribes and depower the tribes. It was part of an actual genocide. The progeny that resulted from the Mexican slaves brought up to work in the missions with the local Chumash were called Mestizo, Mexican and Chumash.

At the time this was going on, there was also a bounty on the Chumash, and to collect the bounty, you had to bring in two Chumash ears to collect one bounty. As a result, the Chumash took on Spanish surnames to hide from what was going on with this dual-pronged genocide. In time, as missionization progressed, and we went into acquiring California into the United States, and the reservation program was built, we put a lot of these Chumash, who were primarily Mestizo, onto reservations, the closest one being the mission reservation at Santa Ynez.

That's the backstory on Chumash development. Most of my Chumash friends said that when the reservation process took place, the people that were actually still Chumash disseminated through the coastal region and remain there in different places to this day.

Robert Lundahl

Well, we have some really interesting contrasts when, you know, we read the papers about what Chumash people are doing, and one of the things that they're doing is building canoes, which they call Tomol, and they're plank canoes, so back to your water history and expertise, and these have been used for a thousand years, so we hear, but we don't really know. I mean, a lot of these sites that we're talking about, like the one on Santa Rosa Island under the Vail Ranch House, that's a lithic tool site that they found, and it's dated at a minimum 8,500 years, perhaps up to 13,000 years of presence there.

David Pu'u

Yep, yep.

Burro Flats, Arrow of Light, Winter Solstice

The theory was there was a land bridge connecting all the islands. It's really interesting when you look back over the geologic span of time in this region, you can see how we had ocean everywhere at one point. There's a place inland from here in Ventura where one of my Chumash friends took me when we were in the middle of that very long drought, and there's a whale pod inland about 10 miles, 12 miles inland from the coast, so we were up there one day looking at the whale pod, and he said, oh, by the way, the

Santa Barbara Museum of Natural History actually got ahold of some of the relics from this whale pod, and we're trying to get them back, and I asked him, I said, what do you want to do? And he goes, well, we want to put them back where they took them in the first place. You're not supposed to take relics and remove them. All that stuff's sacred, so that's the tenet, you know, that Chumash have in common with a lot of the other indigenous people. There are elements within what we call the biome that they consider to be sacred as part of their home.

The Tomol thing is very fascinating because the Chumash tribes that were located in this region, generally you would find a tribe around a coastal waterway. On one side of the stream or river would be one tribe, on the other side would be another. In this region, they were using the pitch, also known as asphaltum, from the oil seeps to seal the Tomols, to seal, you know, cooking utensils, everything. It was an integral part of their culture. They also used it as fuel for fires. So that's how the whole Tomol thing took place and how they sealed the canoes.

They're an ocean tribe. They're an ocean people.

Tomol Plank Canoe, Chumash Tomol Crossing, Channel Islands National Park, U.S. National Park Service

Windmill Blades Can't be Recycled, Pile up in Landfills

Robert Lundahl

So what can we understand and learn from that today when we look at the wind farm and the development and this seemingly contrary value system of sacredness and belonging to place and respect for biodiversity and lifeways and species? What are your general thoughts here? How do we reconcile this?

David Pu'u

Well, I mean, my dad was an engineer. He was a design system failure analyst. I always think that you should really approach the systems that are being proposed from an engineering standpoint.

And I think the goal of each system needs to be that they do not impinge the ecosystems that are placed within, and they need to be economically as well as environmentally sustainable systems. You want projects that make sense and are cradle-to-cradle projects, which means that the items you're using to build the project only also fulfill the needs of society and culture, but do not damage and take away from the system they're placed within. And, you know, that's a question I really have about these wind farms.

I know a lot of my friends that are marine biologists are pretty adamantly opposed to them. I can't say I'm adamantly opposed to it. I don't think I see them as being sustainable in terms of energy production.

I think there's a lot of risk there, but I wouldn't say I'm adamantly opposed to them. There are things about them that I just don't know.

Robert Lundahl, Filmmaker, Journalist

The maintenance requirements are incredibly high. You have to tow these things back, you know, into shore, and you have to say, oh, well, you know, the tower is unsafe now, you know, or the floating tower has been compromised by corrosion or other, you know, salts or those kinds of things. And so the tower needs to come back and get refurbished.

The blades need to get refurbished. And these are huge, right? So as we started discussing earlier, a lot of the stuff that was, you know, preliminary assembly in San Francisco and the port and then towed down to Los Angeles, back up to Morro Bay.

And so this isn't a lightweight matter. This is a little like NASA, and having the launch vehicle on the platform. How does that impact this idea of sustainability?

David Pu'u

Well, I mean, when you look at the potential for this being sustainable, you have to look at the structure itself, the cost to install it, the cost to maintain it. But you have to look, as you do a risk mitigation analysis, at the environment it's being placed into. On top of it being a marine environment, which is typically hazardous to that type of development, based on its chemistry, you have the meteorological problems and the marine weather problems.

That is an extremely active, dynamic area of the coast. In our operations with K-38 Rescue, we're doing training offshore there on a pretty regular basis. And that harbor closes out, that ocean out there goes incredibly dynamic.

Shawn, my boss in K-38 Rescue, told me a story one day about a spot up coast from there at Half Moon Bay, where they were out with one of our instructors, Jonathan Cahill, doing rescue oversight of the surfers out this one big day. And in the middle of all of this, surf kept getting bigger and bigger. They looked out to sea and they saw what they thought was a fog bank.

Big Day, Mavericks, Half Moon Bay, California

And then they realized it was a wave train breaking an open ocean. And it wasn't a fog bank, it was white water in the middle of the ocean. So we're using Kawasaki jet skis and pinned at that point, I think they top out at about 60, 65 knots.

So they pinned the throttle, headed out to sea looking for deep water, and they barely cleared this set of waves. And people call it the 100 foot day, but in looking at where the waves impacted on the headland at Half Moon Bay, we think the wave train may have been in excess of 150 feet. Now, Sean told me that afterwards, after the wave passed, that the wave train closed out the entire Half Moon Bay.

And I don't know if you've ever been there, but it's a massive bay. And it's also a sanctuary area, coincidentally. But after the wave closed out, the ocean was completely calm, there wasn't a single wave, and the ocean was just softly undulating.

Later, in the telemetry system that's set up on top of the cliffs there for the military, they found fish and marine life at in the middle of the military installation, which is, I think, 165 foot elevation. Now imagine if you had a wind farm out there, what would that do? It'd be gone.

So, placing a wind farm in a highly dynamic marine environment has got some risks that people may not be aware of that are involved in the planning.

Robert Lundahl

We were talking about the solar development as another example of renewable implementation in the desert. And I remember a site called Ford Dry Lake, which was being developed by Florida Power and Light, a non-California company, and they were building concentrating solar out there. And they call it Ford Dry Lake, not because it's dry, but because it's a lake.

And water, for years, would run out of these beautiful canyons and these remote, unseen areas full of culture and petroglyphs and artifacts, and just a surprising and

Flood Damage at Ford Dry Lake, Courtesy Basin and Range Watch

unknown area, but a place obviously that supported habitation because of the canyons and the water, and then eventually the runoff of that water into the lake, where they fished as late as the 1970s. But then flash forward to year 2010, and in their wisdom, Florida Power and Light decides to build a solar site out there. So, guess what happened?It flooded. And they thought, okay, we better send a plane up to go look at the flooding and see what the damage and the problem is. So, the plane went up and had problems and crashed, and two people were killed.

And so, that was a mistake based on essentially not knowing where you are. We've seen this before with renewable technologies, and for all the goodwill we have toward the potential solutions, how do we begin to comprehend the variables and the issues and the impact of nature?

David Pu'u

Right. I've been out there to do film work around some of these solar installations, and the scale is massive. And I can't imagine the long-term impact those systems are going to have on the biomes in that region.

I can only see it being negative, actually. I mean, you look at what they're doing, these giant reflective umbrellas blocking light from this massive stretch of land. What does that do to the biome there?

Probably nothing good. And that's without even touching on the efficiency of the solar panels they're installing for that period of technology, as that stuff keeps advancing really rapidly. And we all know there's really no way to recycle those systems, which when it comes back, if you take it back to the wind farm system and the EU, specifically Germany's experience with developing and utilizing these systems, they age out.

And these systems themselves, the physical structures, there's no real way to recycle them. They're polyester chemical. So they've been disassembling these systems as they age out, confessing to the fact that it didn't really meet their power need, that it increased the cost to the consumer.

And then they took the systems over to Africa, where disposal was unregulated and created a landfill, buried the old wind generators in Africa. And that's really an environmental crime.

Chapter Nine- The Economics of Greenwash Clifford Humphrey

Clifford Humphrey started Ecology Action Recyclers in Berkeley in 1968.

He is one of the true founders of the Environmental Movement. Here, he carries a message from the inspired elders who conceived of a better world in the midst of war and chaos like we have today. We began a general conversation about the economics of greenwash, which we circled and snuck up on from behind in this, Clifford's gift to us all.

Clifford Humphrey

Well, I'm going to state to you what's been on my mind here for a few days. I wanted to start with my favorite bumper sticker at UC Berkeley. It was ***economic growth is capital punishment*** and then let you ask questions off of that.

Adam Smith's Emergent Rules of Justice

Robert Lundahl, Filmmaker, Journalist

Well, it leads right into my first question which was to be something like, "How is greenwash financed?

That's one way of entering the conversation, but basically the creation of a false economy around certain ideas that appear to be prosperous or people want to go for because they're into making profit and they don't know too much about anything else.

But there's this whole *hoo-ha*, you know that gets built up around things. It's the *Tulip Economy*. But we apply it to things like, you know, EV batteries, solar power, all these things that can be really good, you know, but unfortunately because you know, the world's markets get focused on that.

There's a great deal of pressure, you know, to come up with the goods, you know, with the mine. You know, the mine is okayed at that point, you know, so yeah, I'll hand it back to you. Is that kind of homing in on the idea?

Clifford Humphrey

Yes. I can go there, but where that takes us, where economic growth and capital punishment, as I said earlier, greenwashing won't feed us. Greenwashing won't solve any of the geopolitical problems that we have now, if anything, might make them a bit worse as countries try harder for their perceived share.

So the talking for me from Thanksgiving to coming out of Black Friday has left me with an absolute determination to speak what's at the core of my activism. And that is this matter of why I went to school in the first place to study psycholinguistics, you know, trying to understand how a lunp of clay could come to the Merriam-Webster dictionary. So what I will put before you, and you can do with it, I respect your field as a filmmaker, and you will do with it.

I am not only suggesting, I wish to say that if I could, if I had the magic wand to do it, I would get all the tanks parked, all of the destroyers at dockside, and all the bombers landed, and all of the atomic bombs in storage, and bring about a world pause to kick off 2024. We have nothing on the agenda in front of us, except how in the world do we come to a world at ease. I don't like the word peace so much, you know, it's kind of a political world, but I do like the phrase of a planet that is at ease with itself.

And so I think we're smart enough to do that. And I think once we bring back, pull back the military budget, we'll have the money to do the right thing. So in some way, we have on the face of the earth now, an opportunity due to all the, you could even say bear traps we've been stepping into, to turn this thing around and have a new day before us of peace.

Militarization in Germany

Because the greenwashing, you know, is focused on consumption, and more consumption is just not going to be the answer. It's already been written that we need another planet to stand by just offshore to harvest. Well, what good is that going to be?

When are we going to need the third one? So as one of my guys, as you know, Buckminster Fuller said, we have to learn to do more with less. That is the absolute truth of it.

We have to take pride in our family's ability, in our sons' and daughters' ability to take us on this road of doing more with less. And so you could say that I got a sailor's cap on because I'm ready to go on this new voyage. We're going to take this voyage to doing more with less.

And you might notice a different temper in my voice before other interviews and this one. So this comes from my soul and my heart. And remember, there was a thing called Citizens Assembly.

There was a thing called People's Parliament. So we've dreamed of this before. You know, we've dreamed of this a long time.

Deliberative Democracy: Citizens' assemblies within government

And so I know it's not only in the air, but it's in our minds and our hearts, and somewhere in all the folders and graduate education departments in all the universities, you know, that there is this possibility of turning the world into a collection of citizens of different countries, and they're all at ease with themselves and with each other. So I would be encouraging, you could say metaphorically, for all armies, all the soldiers of all armies and the officers to take a moment, you know. What's that one famous statue like?

You know, we got a guy with his head down thinking about it. I submit he's thinking about how in the world can we ever come to a time of peace? I'll use the word, however, I like the term *at ease* better.

Even truck drivers on a schedule that are hooked up with satellites to keep track of them. Well, that's not being at ease. They should let them drop off at the Anne's house at least once a week, you know.

You see what I'm getting at? We're on the clock, we're being pushed, and nobody's happy. Just read the paper.

It's almost like journalists have been unleashed this last week. It's amazing, and on the internet they've done polls, and nobody's happy at work anymore. They're just not having a good time, and they take scientific studies of trying to figure out why, and they don't get any answers.

It's just a general demise, and so I will submit to you that we need each other's attention. We need each other's ears and hugs and congratulations, and there's something very important about our ambiance, if you will, our spirit sides intermixing and glowing and coming together. We need to be working together, whatever the definition is.

Ekklesiasterion. The Athenian amphitheater where the Assembly met was an optimized reputation system

“Software is eating the world”, says Marc Andreessen. It is also eating politics. Digital disintermediation affects representative democracy, where the representants are in the position of intermediaries. Thanks to the Internet, there is no technical obstacle for citizens to discuss and vote on every subject.
-Medium

I know there's some people employed, and they just have to go to work one day a week, or some people can be blessed with a few days a month at work, and that really suits them if they have a family to raise. Other times, we need to be a team. We have to really be a team and feel for our place in that team, and so the environmental movement that I took part in, I accepted the journalist boxing up and labeling me of what I was, but I was not an environmentalist.

I was not a pacifist. I was a steward, if you will. I was the steward of the life of this planet's metabolism.

There's something about that that's very sacred. All the aboriginal tribes understood it. We like to show the primitive savages dancing in rhythm in the dust and waving their spears, but without a clue of what their beliefs were,

There are, thankfully, a few anthropologists who were accepted and got to the core of it,

We've been finding out that they were ***dancing for the spirit world***, and so we've come a long way.

We've come a long way, and now it's time to pause. I'm submitting for next year. I'm just around the corner.

My birthday, by the way, happens to be January 11, 1937, so I am going to make a last. I know I'm in my final decade for sure. I'm putting a last decade of my life into this effort to give the world a shake, if you will, and say, look here.

This is ridiculous. How can we spend multi-billions of dollars on a single jet aircraft when 10 or 20 million would be so much elsewhere? It just doesn't make any sense anymore, and I think we're beginning to realize that.

It's like we've backed into an obstruction. We backed into a limitation, but we haven't turned around yet to see what it is, so maybe I can do some good by promoting others who are with me. I know I'm not alone.

I know that. Call me a dreamer, if you will, but that's another bumper sticker. I'm a dreamer, but I'm not alone, so we know.

You know, Robert, we know, so that's my stand for today, you might say, but I will also say that the youth of my recycling efforts in Modesto, they really like to come by and see

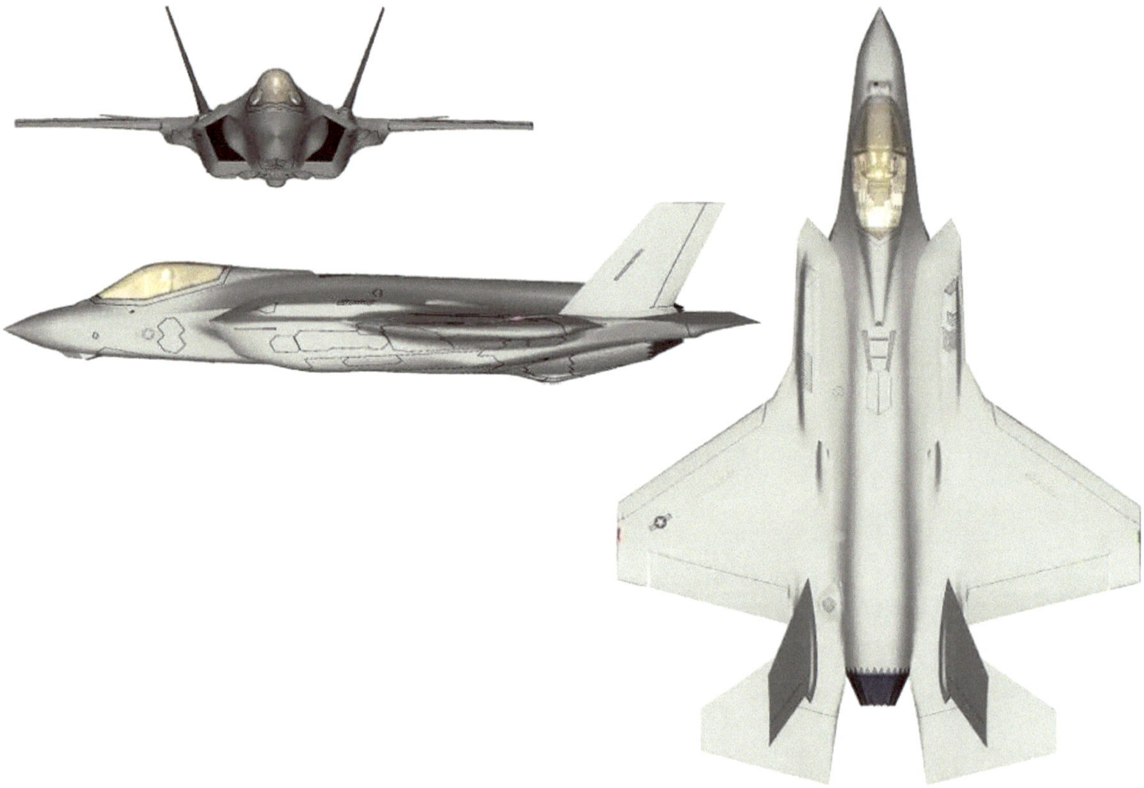

F-35, Forbes, Illustration

the activity. They were seeing the recycling efforts of our curbside programs. They just love to break the bottles.

They love to understand magnetism. We had a magnetic head pulley on a conveyor, and that would separate the metal cans from the aluminum cans, and they would just come up there, skid their bikes to a stop, listen to it, and see the aluminum cans drop off the belt right away, and then the tin cans would come off later, you know, and then we tried to do a three-way split so that the belt was fast enough. It would project the bottles ahead, and then the tin cans would stick on and come around, and then the aluminum cans would drop free, and it worked good if they were dry, and I think that's part of the problem.

What happened with us sending all our goods to China? They were wet and moldy, and they stuck together because the labels started dissolving off the cans and bottles, so we sent them garbage, but we knew how to do it better, and I think the programs are all going to go to a multi-container, and so we can do better. Well, that's an insight of what can apply to this matter of how do we ever get to a world at ease.

We can apply ourselves. I think the answers are right there for our learning. We have to make the effort.

Magnetic Separator for Aluminum Cans

We have to decide that's the goal. We've all accepted our sons are going to be of a certain age. They're going to have to register, and they may have to go off and serve time, if not go into a conflict, but I would say I would plead with everyone coming up this new year.

Go ahead. We'll have a blowout. We've already spent some money on the parties, you know, for New Year's Day, okay, but then that's a sign-off.

Make that a sign-off. We're going to go into a time of ease, at ease with ourselves. A lot of us blame themselves.

I blamed myself, kind of the fear of success thing for a while. I enjoyed doing the work of it, but I couldn't stand up there and take credit. I just always had little short speeches about to do, you know, just do the best you can.

Get a hold of a piece of it you enjoy doing, and do that, and do the best you can. We'll see you all next month, you know. That's about what I would say, but I've learned now that we have people who, I don't know what it is, the ***visionaries, leaders***, whatever that is, that people have standouts for us.

Buckminster Fuller, Courtesy Wired

I'm so embarrassed to use the example, but how in the world did Alexander the Great ever get coined for what he did? It was only because he was famous at 21, or I think he died at 21. He was just famous as a young man.

Well, look what he did. Look what he did. We don't say, back up and take the bull by the horn, you know.

I considered making notes for today, and I didn't make any notes. I just wanted to speak to you all as straightforwardly as I could. Wouldn't everyone prefer to live in a world without the threat of nuclear bombs hanging over them, if the government does the right thing?

My goodness. I don't think, whatever you want to identify as a creator, all that has gone into creating this wonderful planet before us, mountains, water. Oh my goodness, how important is it?The first thing we do, we get off this planet, we go looking for water. We know how important it is. Right now, we're de-icing the planet.

It changes the temperature of the atmosphere. The currents are all going to change. It changes the salinity of the ocean, and on and on and on.

It's not right. This is not a thing to do. It's possible for somebody else who has the same inclination to be a speaker, to be, say, a minister of the planet or future, to get off on this other track of a religious thing, where the creator of the Earth didn't intend this.

Shrinking Greenland Ice Sheet

For heaven's sakes, it's stupidity. We're blowing it up, one chunk after another, and if we don't blow it up, we mine it up, and then throw it in the dump. The dumps are huge piles of resources, and I submit to you that we will probably now, I could learn of a research project somewhere on the planet, of how to take that dump apart and recover all the good stuff from it.

We will probably learn that even there's trace elements hidden away in there that are recoverable, in addition to the metals that are obvious, and then we would end up with organics to be further composted or biologically digested, and then some burning, probably wouldn't we? We could clean it up so we're not putting our batteries, little teeny batteries, in the burner. We could do that.

So there's work to do, and by golly, that equals jobs, right? Work equals jobs. So I'm not pleading for it, but I'm pointing out at some point, we will transfer money from military expenditures to planet stewardship.

I think the environmental movement was good. It gave the journalists, you know, a place in the copy room to argue for their environmental stories, but I think stewardship would have been threatening because it means you're getting more with less. You're out there doing stewardship in the paddocks, in the mountain fields, and so on, making sure when we log, we do it respectfully as well as efficiently, and we don't leave any down broken trees behind us, and we replant.

So the whole budgetary items, you might say, in the budget for humankind on this planet, they will change. They will absolutely change. I've assembled equipment for a podcast, and I still need help putting the wires together, but I will get a helper, and I will have a podcast, and I look forward to talking about this matter of stewardship.

There'll be recorded programs when I start, and I so much enjoyed television at an early age, these talk shows that had guests, and some of the emcees were comical and whatnot. Well, I think I'm going to develop my podcast from recorded shows to having guests. I'll be doing maybe something three or four days a week.

I'm full of it, and I want to get on with the show.

Robert Lundahl, Filmmaker, Journalist

So this idea of stewardship, does stewardship mean that your financial profitability is less or more?

Clifford Humphrey

Well, financial possibility is less, yes. We don't have elders like tribes of Aboriginal people do. I've seen elders work, most notably in the Blackfeet Reservation.

You know, they realize, Montana, they realize they couldn't walk across the Burnover Prairie and have one black foot, so they don't accept our calling them the Blackfoot Reservation, but it's bad English maybe to say Blackfeet Reservation. I don't know why it is. Maybe it just seems off to the map makers, the white map makers.

Anyway, I have seen elders sit. They have days, you might say, of review. They shall come out into the shade or the sunlight, whatever their choice would be, and they sit with their staff, and they receive people.

It's much like some of the things we do in some of our Christian churches, but they're not a minister. They're an elder. They may have done ceremonies in the past and probably did, but there's something magical about being received.

Some Hollywood actors have caught on to this, too, of having a receiving line, but mostly that's not the way that we do it. We seem to be more attracted to huge, raucous audiences, maddening cheering and huge parties with buffet tables with maybe 200 choices of things to eat, and they'll sit in some honored place and watch this extravaganza and a few friends get to talk with them or eat with them. Well, no.

We have to learn to respect our elders. At one point, my wife, Mary Pacey is my first wife. I have been married twice.

My first wife would go to a dog checked over by the vet, a deaf, black Russell, Jack Russell Terrier, a white one, and we'd visit hospitals. Oh, that was wonderful. That was just wonderful.

Yes, there's the hospital surprise of it, the glory of doing a visit like that, but there's also something. I know that many of you, for instance, have fed horses apples over the fence, not having any idea what their name was or who owned them, but I could just hold up an apple over the top of the fence and just make any kind of a noise. Watch the horse's head and the ears would pop up and then come over and feed them the apple.

As you listen to that crunching and swallowing and then them being patient and waiting for a second or a third apple, there's a juncture of some kind to the point that I think now of humanity on the planet as one body, capital B, you know, one Body. Humanity is one Body. This is what we have to heal.

We're trashing our planet where we grew up. I often think of what I like to import grapes year round, and so I have my UN elbow here. I tell the kids, you know, and I ask them just to put their hand on their elbow when I give little talks.

I've given more talks to children than I have to youth clubs, by the way, so I have had youth activism, but I haven't talked to today's 4-H clubs and so on, but kids, their hand on their elbow and ask them, close their eyes and imagine the farthest out molecule or atom, whichever word they like, is on their elbow, and then we talk about where it came from. It's been on a long trip, and I can take them back through that trip all the way back to dinosaurs, adding their calcium in their bones to the ground, which they have on the end of their elbow, and I really wish I could be a fly on the wall when they get home and tell their mom they have a dinosaur on their elbow.

I think that would be a wonderful thing, but that's part of the teaching that we must have to respect life and our bodies and the fact that, yes, death is a natural thing, and we can all get a little help along the way, and then to have some respect, we need something more.

Have you seen those photographs, all of you out there? Have you seen those photographs of military cemeteries, thousands of crosses all lined up perfectly? Does that really honor them in any way?

We need some way of doing that. I don't know what to suggest, but I have imagined a family place where it could be known that everybody that is of that family, what their favorite plant was or what their favorite food was, that's important, you know. He was shot on the beach after he wrote a letter home, couldn't wait to get home to some of Aunt Emma's stew again, something like that, you know, a human note, and we're struggling now as the planet is warming to cool it, and the only specific thing I want to mention is burn less fossil fuels.

All of us, carpools, and this is hard heat on Tier C. We're a little place. You can spend more gas trying to pick people up than if all three drove maybe to their job separately.

There's no real industry to speak of here. We do have the hot water baths, and we still have a few people in the country who like to soak in certain mineral spirits, and some even drink it too. I'm drinking the hot water here in truth to consequences.

Maybe that's why I can carry on as I do. I don't know. But I'm coming up on, I think it's 88 this next January, more than 37.

I guess that'd be right. Anyway, stewardship. This is the word now for the world.

Getting more with less.

Go back and look at Bucky Fuller's work. Take a lesson from him.

Montreal Biosphere, R. Buckminster Fuller, 1967 © Ralf Roletschek

www.ingramcontent.com/pod-product-compliance
Lightning Source LLC
LaVergne TN
LVHW071241210926
848486LV00007B/318

* 9 7 9 8 9 9 5 1 6 6 1 5 3 *